Emotion Focused Family Therapy with Children and Caregivers

This book introduces Emotion Focused Family Therapy (EFFT) as an evidence-based intervention for children through the integration of parent trauma and emotion-focused techniques to facilitate family-based change. A team of expert authors, including founders of EFT and EFFT, contribute to the chapters, in which recent findings from clinical trials are woven into a rich and deeply presented overview of using EFFT practically with clients. This immensely practical book also provides illustrative case studies, intervention strategies or dos and don'ts, and clinical worksheets.

Mirisse Foroughe, PhD, is a clinical psychologist and director of psychological services at Kindercare Psychology, heading the Primary Care Psychology Research Lab. She holds an adjunct faculty position with York University in Toronto and is the primary developer of the EFFT Research Program. Dr. Foroughe has received the Ontario Psychological Association Early Career Psychologist Award and the Canadian Psychological Association's 2017 PFC Innovative Service Award.

Emotion Focused Family Therapy with Children and Caregivers
A Trauma-Informed Approach

Edited by Mirisse Foroughe

NEW YORK AND LONDON

First published 2018
by Routledge
52 Vanderbilt Avenue, New York, NY 10017

and by Routledge
2 Park Square, Milton Park, Abingdon, Oxon, OX14 4RN

Routledge is an imprint of the Taylor & Francis Group, an informa business

© 2018 Taylor & Francis

The right of Mirisse Foroughe to be identified as the author of the editorial material, and of the authors for their individual chapters, has been asserted in accordance with sections 77 and 78 of the Copyright, Designs and Patents Act 1988.

All rights reserved. The purchase of this copyright material confers the right on the purchasing institution to photocopy pages which bear the photocopy icon and copyright line at the bottom of the page. No other part of this publication may be reproduced, stored in a retrieval system, or transmitted in any form or by any means, electronic, mechanical, photocopying, recording or otherwise, without prior permission in writing from the publisher.

Trademark notice: Product or corporate names may be trademarks or registered trademarks, and are used only for identification and explanation without intent to infringe.

Library of Congress Cataloging-in-Publication Data
Names: Foroughe, Mirisse, editor.
Title: Emotion focused family therapy with children and caregivers : a trauma-informed approach / edited by Mirisse Foroughe.
Description: New York, NY : Routledge, 2018. | Includes bibliographical references.
Identifiers: LCCN 2017047105 | ISBN 9781138063358 (hardcover : alk. paper) | ISBN 9781138063365 (pbk. : alk. paper) | ISBN 9781315161105 (e-book)
Subjects: | MESH: Family Therapy | Emotion-Focused Therapy | Psychological Trauma—therapy | Child | Caregivers | Adolescent
Classification: LCC RC455.4.F3 | NLM WM 430.5.F2 | DDC 616.89/156—dc23
LC record available at https://lccn.loc.gov/2017047105

ISBN: 978-1-138-06335-8 (hbk)
ISBN: 978-1-138-06336-5 (pbk)
ISBN: 978-1-315-16110-5 (ebk)

Typeset in Bembo
by Apex CoVantage, LLC

Contents

About the Contributors — vii
Foreword: A Caregiver-Based Intervention — ix

1. **Overview of Emotion-Focused Therapy** — 1
   GENEVIEVE VRANA AND LESLIE GREENBERG

2. **Emotion-Focused Therapies for Children and Adolescents** — 23
   MIRISSE FOROUGHE

3. **Development and Core Components of EFFT** — 45
   MIRISSE FOROUGHE, JOANNE DOLHANTY, PRIYANJALI MITHAL, AND ADÈLE LAFRANCE

4. **Emotion Focused Family Therapy in Practice** — 63
   MIRISSE FOROUGHE AND LAURA GOLDSTEIN

5. **Processing Parent Blocks** — 80
   MIRISSE FOROUGHE AND LAURA GOLDSTEIN

6. **EFFT and Trauma: Engaging the Parent With a Dismissing Attachment Style** — 99
   KRISTINA CORDEIRO, SARA LYNN REPENDA, ROBERT T. MULLER, AND MIRISSE FOROUGHE

7. **Practical Resources** — 120
   MIRISSE FOROUGHE, JOANNE DOLHANTY, AND ADÈLE LAFRANCE

Glossary — 151
Index — 155

Contributors

Kristina Cordeiro is currently a graduate student in the Clinical-Developmental Psychology program at York University in Toronto. Supervised by Dr. Muller, her research and clinical interests lie in intrafamilial trauma and attachment-based treatments. She has over 10 years experience working with children and young families in educational settings and is a trained behavioural therapist.

Joanne Dolhanty, PhD, is a supervising and consulting clinical psychologist and trainer for mental health organizations across Canada and internationally. With Dr. Greenberg she developed the application of Emotion-Focused Therapy to eating disorders, and she is the co-developer of Emotion Focused Family Therapy.

Laura Goldstein has worked under the mentorship of Dr. Foroughe since 2014, learning emotion-focused and related therapies, working with children and families, and conducting clinical research. She is currently an MA candidate in the Clinical-Developmental Psychology Program at York University working under the supervision of Dr. Muller, and her research currently examines nonverbal and paralinguistic indicators of intrafamilial and intergenerational trauma and attachment difficulties. She holds an Honours B.A. from York University and a Diploma in Liberal Arts from Seneca College.

Leslie Greenberg, PhD, is Distinguished Research Professor Emeritus of Psychology at York University, Toronto, and primary developer of Emotion-Focused Therapy. He has published extensively. He has received the American Psychological Association Award for Distinguished Professional Contribution to Applied Research, the Distinguished Research Career Award of the International Society for Psychotherapy Research, and the Carl Rogers Award of the American Psychology Association.

Adèle Lafrance, C. Psych, is a clinical psychologist and Associate Professor in the Psychology Department at Laurentian University, Canada. She is the co-developer of Emotion Focused Family Therapy. Dr. Lafrance provides consultation, supervision, and training for individual clinicians, departments, and organizations worldwide. She is the author of several publications in the field of eating disorders and mental health, and leads multiple projects to promote family-oriented interventions.

Priyanjali Mithal is a graduate student at University of Toronto completing an MSc in the Department of Pharmaceutical Sciences, where she researches psychological interventions to reduce needle pain and fear in adults. She has an Honours BSc in Psychology from York University, and has a long-standing interest in clinical psychology, specifically the therapeutic process and interventions that can help enhance and restore psychological well-being.

Robert T. Muller, PhD, is Fellow of the International Society for the Study of Trauma & Dissociation (ISSTD), Professor at York University, and author of "Trauma & the Avoidant Client," which won the 2011 ISSTD award for the year's best written work on trauma. Lead investigator on several trauma therapy programs, Muller lectures internationally. His online magazine, "The Trauma & Mental Health Report," is visited by over 100,000 readers annually.

Sara Lynn Rependa is a senior doctoral candidate with Dr. Muller in the Trauma & Attachment Lab at York University. Her recent research has focused on therapeutic alliance and treatment response among children in trauma therapy. Her clinical work includes the treatment of adult and child survivors of trauma in both inpatient and outpatient settings.

Genevieve Vrana has trained under the supervision of Dr. Greenberg since 2008. During this time, she has gained expertise in EFT theory, research, and practice. Most recently, she developed a new model for understanding clients' avoidance of their painful emotions, along with a roadmap of how EFT therapists can intervene to help clients overcome their avoidance. She has spoken about her findings at various international conferences.

Foreword: A Caregiver-Based Intervention

"It is easier to build strong children than it is to repair broken men."
—Frederick Douglass

As a beginning therapist, this quote was my mantra. I did not set out to work with adult trauma. I decided to work with kids because they were easier to treat, closer to the root, more amenable to change, and less defended. At least, this is what I thought—and I still believe that the latter three assumptions are true, but the first most certainly is not. Kids are not easier to *treat*, if treating really means supporting someone's transformation from a distressed state to a healthy one. Truly transforming a child's state of mental health necessarily involves—or should involve—the most important people in their lives: parents. And parents are adults, often with long histories of important suffering. So, despite my best efforts, I didn't get away from working with adults at all—I was one step removed, but there they were: in the waiting room, on the answering machine, behind worried emails, wondering how long treatment was going to take, letting me know the "real deal"—all the important (and usually more negative) details that the child left out of our discussions. They were, at the very least, an important source of feedback, and an important part of their child's life. They were also the most important part of the child's larger "system."

After many years of individually based mental health services, in the mid-20th century, family systems theory suggested an alternative to individual therapy, and many child therapists realized that we needed to work with all parts of the system—including the adults in the child's life. Family systems changed things, but for most of us working in children's mental health, the child was still the "identified patient." Indeed, even if we felt that the parents were, in fact, the psychologically distressed ones in the family—sometimes seeing their child through an impaired and distorted lens that mirrored back an image of a child that was intolerable, unparentable, defiant, out-of-control, or otherwise *wrong* in some way—what could we do? We either said nothing about it, and just tried to help the child cope, or we tried to convince parents of how they *should* see, understand, and relate to their child—largely to no avail.

You couldn't start telling parents that *they* were the problem. Well, you *could*, but there would likely be a huge fallout in terms of your rapport with them. Some therapists actually did confront parents in this way, and sometimes they never saw their patient again, and maybe the parent would find another therapist. In my early training, I worked in large school boards, mental health agencies, renowned teaching hospitals, all with many highly gifted and experienced supervising clinicians. Still, not even my supervisors had a way to talk to parents about the things they were doing—or not doing—that were interfering with their child's recovery. We all wanted to be respectful of families and wait for them to come around to understanding things. Humanistic and client-centred approaches told us that people are the experts on their own experience, and the emphasis on following the client in session made it difficult to introduce any bold reflections or controversial insights that would run counter to how parents saw themselves, or wanted to see themselves. So we said nothing to parents even when (especially when) we saw that how they were responding was getting in the way of the child's healing, or somehow contributing to the maintenance of the child's problems.

Sometimes, as a child therapist, one can come to ally very strongly with the child and blame a parent for not seeing what the child needs. In times such as these, there were covert looks of sympathy from the therapist towards the child, nonverbal themes of "you're really okay, sweetie, it's just your parents—hang in there a few more years and you can get out." All of our true clinical impressions would conveniently go right over the parent's head, because they were so busy blaming the child and pointing out all their flaws, unable to see their role in the manufacturing of a diagnosis that was sometimes mere comfort for the adult with a child they simply couldn't manage. And of course, we were so busy blaming parents that we were unable to see how our attitude towards them, both the lack of corrective coaching and the lack of expressed empathy, was creating further divide between parent and child.

Of course, the children wouldn't stay "okay" for long in this environment. The more the message of "something is wrong with you" was mirrored back to the child, through the parent's strong reactions to typical, although sometimes overly sensitive, child behaviour, the more the child came to believe that it was true—something *is* wrong with me. *I am defiant. I am sick. I have problems. I am driving my parents crazy. I am crazy.* Until the child eventually became a shadow of their true potential, usually desperately needing their parent's approval, while defiantly hanging on to the notion that they were *not* crazy and their parents were the ones with the problem, and other times submitting whole-heartedly to the notion that they were sick, troubled, and broken.

Working with these children, I felt helpless and disappointed in myself many times, realizing that I was just a part of this process designed to assuage parents of their distress and shift the blame to a child. In individual sessions with the child, I would try desperately to rebuild their self-esteem, give them a sense of "okayness," and at least one relationship in which they were seen as worthy, healthy, and able to heal. I could sense their confusion, craving the positive image of themselves that they could see in my eyes, but needing to cling to the other image—the one of the troubled child—because regardless of how strong our therapeutic alliance had grown to be, it was not what they truly needed in order to feel whole. I was never going to replace their mother or father or primary caregiver. The trouble was, *I was working on the wrong relationship. The relationship that they needed to feel healthy in was the one with their primary attachment figure(s).* The place they needed to feel whole in was their own home. And the person that they needed on their treatment team was their parent. I could only be the facilitator of this.

Around this time, I had been working on an infant and preschool treatment team at a renowned children's mental health agency in Toronto. Under the supervision of experts in infant mental health, I trained in an approach to dyadic, parent-child play therapy, known as "Watch, Wait, and Wonder" (WWW). In this approach, I was finally the instrument of healing within an existing parent-child relationship, instead of a party in the creation of a secondary relationship that could never quite come close in significance to the original relationship between the child and their primary caregiver. When a child in WWW approached me to show or tell me something, I directed her to the mother or father. The relationship that mattered was theirs—and my relationship with the *parent* was, in dyadic therapy, even more important than the one I would form with the child. Everything in WWW subtly encouraged the parent to take on the role of the healer, the one in tune with the child's needs, the one reflecting on how to meet those needs, and the one deciding which strategies to try, when, and for how long—and knowing when they had found the way that was most healing to that child. I was a witness to a remarkable thing: a parent coming into their own, realizing that they could take full ownership of the relationship between parent and child, and feeling empowered to make all the difference in their child's forming identity, overcoming of obstacles, and mental health. The parent's *belief in their ability to meet their child's needs* was the critical factor, and it was my job to believe it for them until they believed it themselves. My belief in the parent would help restore the parent's own confidence, help repair the parent-child relationship, and protect the child's mental health.

Watch, Wait, and Wonder was the first approach I had learned that envisioned parents as the agent of change and healing for a child. However, the approach also took a long time, often a year of dyadic therapy, and it relied on the parents figuring things out for themselves. Some parents seemed to have beliefs about the child and about themselves that were so firmly entrenched, watching and waiting just didn't work. In those cases, there was no clear way to move past what was getting in the way for parents—if they couldn't see the solution was within their reach, I had to wait for them to see it, and sometimes that came at a high cost to the parent-child relationship and to the child's mental health.

As well, the dyadic, play-based approach of empowering the parent to heal their child ended abruptly at age 6. For 7-year-olds and up, we usually offered individual therapy. There was the option of family therapy, but it wasn't with the same approach: the "client" in the family therapy was the family, and we needed all family members to be willing participants in the therapy process, which was aimed at addressing communication and dynamics within a family. If a 15-year-old presented for therapy, and didn't "want" their parent(s) involved, well, who were we to trample on their right to privacy and their ability to consent to solitary treatment? They were already 15. We could work on preparing them for the transition to adulthood...the transition away from the hope that they could ever get what they needed emotionally from their parents. We could teach them to accept their parent's limitations, to learn to cope with life, show them they would be okay on their own. At least they had us, the therapists, for as long as the therapy lasted. And then they would have themselves, their friends, and the rest of the world. It was the best we could do, but was it best for the child?

Throughout the individual therapy process for a child, parents would typically be ever grateful that their child had "a safe place to talk," clearly feeling that they could not offer that safe place, and they were not capable of taking on their child's needs. This is the reason they needed our professional help. We were the experts. Somehow their child had lost their way (and of course every parent actually blamed themselves for that, although only a few talked about it openly), and we were going to take the child's needs out of their uncertain hands, into our capable ones, and do a better job than they could. This was the implicit message, made explicit in some models of care as a "parentectomy."

Other parents would remain sceptical of the work we were doing (which was a mystery to them, as they were excluded from it almost entirely), with some parents even doubting the utility of therapy, and convinced that we were "fuzzy, cuddly therapists taking the child's side" and not seeing what the child was really like. Sometimes, these parents would stop bringing the child mid-therapy or would have a hard time managing the initial and middle phases of therapy, when emotional distress often increases, and would end up seeking out medication for the child without allowing therapy a chance to work.

And if things did go fairly well, and we formed a strong therapeutic alliance with their child, the parent tolerated us because their child had a place to vent, so the family could function as it had been functioning and *the parent would not have to deal with the child's inability to deal.* We gave them tools, now they could deal. It was good enough. We didn't quite "fix" their child as they had hoped we would, but we bandaged them up good enough to get by, do better in school, argue less at home, and seem to be in a better mood. These were important indicators of good functioning, so there you go. Here's your kid back, a little better than when you gave them to us. And the parent's sense of competence? Had that changed? Did they feel any of the empowerment that the parents in dyadic play therapy had felt? Not at all—how could they? The agent of change was the clinician-child therapeutic relationship: we had some secret way of connecting with their child that they could never have. And it *was* all a secret: the child had a right to privacy after all. We all colluded in this massive parentectomy. The parent gave the child to an expert healer and was, at best, appreciative that someone could reach this child, because they most certainly couldn't be the ones to do it. Right? Wrong.

There was no other condition for which this model failed more miserably than for eating disorders. And, as it turned out, there was perhaps no other condition for which a parental sense of competence was more critical than for eating disorders. With a child at the doorstep of death, refusing the very medicine she desperately needed, it was not the knowledge and technique of the expert but the power of the parent armed with this knowledge and technique that would ultimately, the evidence clearly showed, heal the child and give her a chance at life again.

When parents were engaged in family-based treatment (FBT) using the Maudsley FBT approach, the recovery rates for children would increase from the mid-30s to the mid-80s—without relapse—changing the course of a condition that had previously come to be known as a "chronic, relapsing disorder." Coach parents to become the nurses, we were surprised to discover, and the child would heal and stay healed long after leaving the hospital. This realization changed my career, and changed the very topic of my doctoral dissertation two years after I had set out to show why it was that people with restricting eating disorders could not be healed. To know that treatment success could be increased so drastically just by helping the parents take the driver's seat—it was a new paradigm. Yet it made so much sense.

But why stop at eating disorders? Clinicians were now offering family-based treatment to people with EDs, but kids with anxiety or depression or social difficulties were still being treated as solo projects, identified patients, black sheep, the "problem child" that needed to be extracted, fixed, and then sent back to function within the family. Even the most well-intentioned "family-based" approaches, such as family therapy for a child's anxiety disorder, retained the idea of the therapist as expert on healing the child rather than empowering parents to see the healing as their role to own.

But what's wrong with that? Why not get the parents on board by teaching and instructing and leave it at that? *Because it does not include the child's primary caregivers as agents of change and healing, and does not offer parents any real support in becoming a primary agent.* Without the complete shift from blaming parents, ignoring parents, or instructing parents to empowering parents, there can be no real transformation, no increase in the parent's own sense of parenting efficacy. In times of need, the child learns to wait to speak with the therapist until therapy ends, and then learns to hide in plain sight, turn to coping mechanisms, and try to need less from their parents.

With the messaging that their parents cannot meet their emotional needs, the core of the child's pain remains. And the child learns to cope with that pain for a few months, or maybe even a few years if the strategies that we teach them helped them become quite adept at containing their intense, negative emotions. Nonetheless, eventually, inevitably, the emotions rise up and drown them, or catch them off guard, and boom—sometimes at last arriving at the eating disorder diagnosis.

It was as if the earlier cries were just not loud enough to be heard, and it was going to take the ultimate psychiatric diagnosis: the disorder with the highest mortality rate, so gripping that the child loses their ability to cope on their own or to sustain life on their own. The founders of EFFT heard these helpless cries, both the child's helplessness and the parent's, and found a brilliant way to acknowledge and process the parent's painful emotions in the service of healing the child's eating disorder. EFFT provided parents with the confidence they needed in order to heal their own child ... in the process often embarking on a journey of healing for themselves and the whole family as well.

For other kids, it would be self-harm, suicidal behaviour, or addiction that would sound the battle cry. For some others still, nothing seemed to be enough, and the family's ability to avoid facing the child's emotions was so powerful, so entrenched, and so seemingly necessary for their own sense of "okayness" that the child would self-destruct before their eyes, while the family held on to the notion that they could do nothing to save them. At those times, I felt so angry, so disappointed in the families—*I thought of them as families who had failed their child.*

But wait. Had the family failed? And if they had failed, on who's watch? What was my role in all of this? It took years to see that it was I—the therapist—who had failed. It was *my* role to believe in the family's ability to heal itself and its members until the family believed it too. If I didn't do that, could I rightly blame the family for not believing in themselves?

As a fourth year Honour's student, I had conducted research on the power of expectancy effects: the tendency for someone to live up or down to what is expected of them. But these powerful effects are not limited in influence to children. Adults can be transformed by the expectations of others as well. If I don't tell a parent what they could do to help their child, am I not assuming that they are incapable of doing it? Unreachable. Unhelpable. What kind of helping professional believes that a huge segment of the population—parents of children with mental health challenges—can't be helped along? Do parents not look to us as professionals to guide them in the process of change and healing for their child? Why do we clinicians hold back from explicitly telling parents—just as clinicians tell parents of children with eating disorders, with the utmost compassion and absence of finger-pointing—that *parents are the most powerful agent of change*? It isn't about what *caused* the child's problems, but about *"how are we going to get the child to be rid of this problem?"* How can we obliterate what is standing in their way? And how do we empower parents to take responsibility in their child's recovery *not because they are to blame, but because they are irreplaceable?* The answer to these and all similar questions is: Bring in the parents!

The Parent's Role in Healing Their Child

In this approach, we believe that parents are the solution to the problems gripping their child, regardless of the cause. The process of helping their child through it will only strengthen their bond, as the child comes to see that their parent can catch them, hold them, and propel them back out into the world stronger and more prepared. If a child falls off their bike when you are first teaching them to ride, would you stand back and allow someone else to help them up because someone told you that there is a guy there in the park that is an expert at helping up wounded kids? No! You would run and grab your child and lift them up and tend to their wounds, and just when you knew they were almost ready, you would encourage them back onto the bike, tuning out the rest of the world and taking a chance but letting them know that you believe they can do it! You wouldn't let anyone take your place as that child begins to ride the bike again, just as when she was a baby and took her first steps. You want to be there and be part of it. Years later, your child might even say, "Thanks for always being there for me." Or they might not. The point is, they sense that they have you to turn to and count on, and this counts for a lot in the world of attachment security.

Healing a child's emotional wounds is always within a parent's scope of ability. They are the things that children are *supposed* to look to a parent for. Emotional wounds are best healed by those closest to you, with whom you have the strongest attachment. *A therapist will never be as powerful as a parent with the same skill set.* Once parents realize that they have the skills, there is no comparison between them and a secondary relationship with someone completely insignificant in the child's actual life, history, and neurobiology. It may sting a bit, particularly for those of us having derived our sense of identity from being the "savers of the lost child." But now we can be the "healers of the lost relationship," setting in motion the most protective, the most natural, and the most enduring bond: *the bond between parent and child.* It will also be a gift, this facilitating of the healing process within a primary relationship, to the children and families with whom we have the honour to work. We will be the conduit. And that uneasy feeling of taking an already lost child even further away from their own parents will be gone forever.

So how to do this? A good start is to explicitly convey to the parents that they are important—*critical, necessary, powerful*—in their child's recovery. And then to coach them in the *how* of becoming involved in the recovery process, which almost always involves finding out their weak spots and strengthening them so that they can present their strongest, most capable, confident, and competent self to the child. In this work, another simple yet powerful idea can be a guide:

> "The best way out is always through."
> —Robert Frost

If we want to help parents out, we have to help them through. Through their insecurities, through their self-blame, and through their own pain. Parents are in pain, too. They have current pain from their child's difficulties, and older pain from their own childhoods. Often, that old pain can get in the way of dealing with the child's current needs. They need our support to get through that pain, to work through whatever the blocks might be—and this can seem like a huge task to us, the child therapists who (for whatever reason—but maybe important to think about) decided only to work with the "easier to treat" children . . . because children are so honest, so open, so wanting to heal. But what do children need most? What do they need to feel in times of distress? Of course, it's to know *that they could turn to their parents in times of need.* This is the core of attachment theory: the baby cries until the loving parent soothes the cries. This is the most powerful healing that a human can experience: to see one's own parents as the image of strength and love so that the child feels so supported that there is no doubt they can make it. Even if the child feels unbearably weak, the parent can catch them if they fall. The parent will not break. The parent will not run. The parent will not cower. In the face of the seemingly powerful "illness," "disorder," "addiction," or "problem," the parent will be an even stronger power, and the force of their love, persistence, and sheer will to save the child will be exactly the medicine that the child needs in order to heal. Now let us get out there and invite those parents in from the waiting room.

Mirisse Foroughe

1 Overview of Emotion-Focused Therapy

Genevieve Vrana and Leslie Greenberg

An Evidence-Based Treatment

Emotion-Focused Therapy (EFT) is recognized as an evidence-based treatment for depression and marital distress (Elliott, Greenberg, & Lietaer, 2004; Johnson, Greenberg, & Schlindler, 1999). It has also demonstrated positive outcomes for trauma (Paivio & Nieuwenhuis, 2001; Paivio & Pascual-Leone, 2010), eating disorders (Robinson, Dolhanty, & Greenberg, 2015; Robinson, Dolhanty, Stillar, Henderson, & Mayman, 2014; Wnuk, Greenberg, & Dolhanty, 2015), anxiety disorders (MacLeod, Elliott, & Rodgers, 2012; Shahar, Bar-Kalifa, & Alon, 2017; Watson & Greenberg, 2017), and interpersonal problems (Greenberg & Malcolm, 2002; Greenberg, Warwar, & Malcolm, 2008; Paivio & Greenberg, 1995). A manualized form of EFT for depression was found to be highly effective in treating depression in three separate clinical trials (Goldman, Greenberg, & Angus, 2006; Greenberg & Watson, 1998, 2006; Watson, Gordon, Stermac, Kalogerakos, & Steckley, 2003). In these trials, EFT was as or more effective than a client-centred (CC) empathic treatment or a cognitive behavioural treatment (CBT). Both CBT and CC were highly successful in reducing depression; however, EFT was more effective in reducing interpersonal problems than either of the two other treatments, along with promoting more improvement in symptoms, compared to the CC treatment. Further, EFT was highly successful in preventing relapse over an 18-month follow-up period (77% non-relapse; Ellison, Greenberg, Goldman, & Angus, 2009).

EFT has generated a lot of research on the process of change—possibly more than any other treatment approach. Several therapy process variables have been found to contribute significantly to therapeutic outcome in EFT, namely: therapist empathy, therapeutic alliance, client depth of experiencing, emotional arousal, making sense of aroused emotion, productive emotional processing, and particular emotion sequences (e.g., Boritz, Angus, Monette, Hollis-Walker, & Warwar, 2011; Choi, Pos, & Magnusson, 2016; Elliott et al., 2004; Goldman, Greenberg, & Pos, 2005; Greenberg, Auszra, & Herrmann, 2007; Malin & Pos, 2015; Missirlian, Toukmanian, Warwar, & Greenberg,

2005; Pascual-Leone & Greenberg, 2007; Pos, Greenberg, Goldman, & Korman, 2003; Tarba, 2015; Wong & Pos, 2014).

Theoretical Underpinnings

EFT is a humanistic-integrative approach that emphasizes the importance of human emotion in psychological functioning and therapeutic change. With early roots in humanistic, Gestalt, and existential therapies (Frankl, 1959; May, 1977; Perls, Hefferline, & Goodman, 1951; Rogers, 1957; Yalom, 1980), as well as family systems theory (Bowen, 1966; Pascual-Leone, 1987), EFT later drew on advances in cognitive neuroscience and emotion research (Damasio, 1999; Frijda, 1986; Izard, 2002; Tamietto & de Gelder, 2010). In this context, EFT theory and practice were developed through several years of research into the process of therapeutic change (Greenberg, 1986, 2002; Greenberg & Johnson, 1988; Greenberg, Rice, & Elliott, 1993; Greenberg & Safran, 1987; Rice & Greenberg, 1984).

Although EFT uses an integrative framework, there is a sustained focus on a person's emotions. An emphasis on experiential engagement and felt emotions is seen as the primary vehicle of change. In EFT, a person needs to experience their painful feelings in order to change them; in other words, they have to arrive at a place before leaving it (Greenberg, 2012).

Research has shown that emotional experiences are fundamentally adaptive to human functioning. Emotions can and often do occur earlier and more quickly than cognitions, and they make an integral contribution to information processing (LeDoux, 1996; Greenberg, 2011; Forgas, 1995, 2000; Greenberg, 2002; Greenberg & Safran, 1987). Moreover, people rely on emotion as a foundation for many cognitive processes, particularly for making decisions (Bechera, Damasio, Tranel, & Damasio, 1997; Damasio, 1994).

Emotions are connected to our most essential needs, rapidly alerting us to situations that are important to our well-being and ensuring that we are prepared for action (Damasio, 2003; Frijda, 1986; Greenberg, 2004; Izard, 2002; Tomkins, 1962). For example, fear can quickly alert us to danger, making sudden escape possible; anger can signal that our boundaries have been violated, promoting an assertive response; sadness or grief can indicate a loss, encouraging us to seek comfort and support from others. More "positive" emotions, such as joy and contentment, tell us that we are safe, that threats to our survival are absent, and that we can let our guard down.

People form associations between lived experiences and the emotions evoked at the time, creating emotional memories. In other words, people react from their emotion systems, not only to biologically inherited cues of danger and safety, but also to learned associations, such as a parent's impatient voice or the tune of a soothing lullaby (Greenberg, 2011). In EFT, these emotional memories form a part of organizing networks referred to as *emotion schemes* (Oatley, 1992; Greenberg et al., 1993; Greenberg & Paivio, 1997).

Emotion schemes involve several elements: 1) *situational-perceptual* experiences, including immediate appraisals of current situations and emotionally charged memories, such as noticing that you are alone or isolated from others and remembering an experience of abandonment from childhood; 2) *bodily sensations and expressions*, such as tightness in the chest or a sinking feeling in the stomach; 3) *implicit verbal-symbolic* representations, including self-labels (e.g., "unlovable"); and 4) *motivation-behavioural* elements, including needs and action tendencies like wanting closeness with others or withdrawing from contact (Elliott & Greenberg, 2017). Exposure to any of the above elements of an emotion scheme can quickly and automatically re-activate the entire scheme. For example, a present-day situation that bears resemblance to an earlier experience of rejection can serve as a cue to re-activate old, familiar feelings of sadness and hopelessness. This means that people can re-experience an emotional memory many times long after the original event. These kinds of emotional experiences are the main targets of intervention in EFT.

Distinguishing Between Different Kinds of Emotions

While EFT acknowledges that emotions are adaptive to human survival and well-being, emotional processes can become problematic as a result of past trauma or even ongoing misattunement between a person's emotional needs and what is available in their environment (McGuinty et al., 2015). Consequently, emotion-focused therapists use a system of in-session process diagnosis to differentiate between types of emotional responses and intervene accordingly (Greenberg & Paivio, 1997; Greenberg & Watson, 2006; Elliott et al., 2004). In this system of sorting out the client's emotions, an important distinction is made between primary and secondary emotions. *Primary emotions* are a person's most fundamental, direct initial reactions to a situation, such as being sad at a loss or angry at a boundary violation. *Secondary emotions*, on the other hand, are responses to a person's own thoughts or feelings rather than to the situation. For example, feeling angry in response to feeling hurt by someone, or feeling guilty about feeling angry.

EFT's emotion diagnostic system also distinguishes between primary states that are adaptive and those that are maladaptive (Greenberg & Goldman, 2007; Greenberg & Watson, 2006). *Primary adaptive* emotion responses are a person's first, natural reactions to the current situation that would help them take appropriate action (Greenberg, 2010). For example, if a person is being violated by someone, anger is an adaptive response, because it helps them take assertive action to end the violation. Another example of an adaptive emotional response is sadness over a loss, which motivates the person to seek connection. In contrast, *primary maladaptive* emotions are less reliable guides for action. They are the old, familiar feelings that occur repeatedly and do not change over time, such as a core sense of loneliness and anxious insecurity or a feeling of worthlessness and inadequacy that plagues a person throughout their life (Greenberg, 2010). These maladaptive feelings do not shift in response to changes in circumstance and they also do not provide adaptive directions for solving problems when they are experienced.

For therapeutic change to occur, primary adaptive emotions need to be accessed for their adaptive information and ability to organize helpful action, whereas maladaptive emotions need to be accessed, regulated, and transformed into more adaptive emotional responses (Greenberg, 2010, 2011). As well, secondary emotions need to be bypassed so that the primary emotions underlying them can be accessed and used in the healing process (Elliott et al., 2004).

A third category of emotions is *instrumental emotions*. These are strategic displays of emotion for their intended effect on others, such as feigning sadness to receive the comfort of others (Elliott & Greenberg, 2017; Greenberg & Watson, 2006). Common examples include "crocodile tears" (instrumental sadness), "crying wolf" (instrumental fear), and displays of intimidation (instrumental anger). Instrumental emotions may be expressed deliberately out of habit or automatically without full awareness. Therapists need to gently and empathically help clients become aware of the effects of and intentions behind expressing these emotions, so that clients may find more direct ways of expressing themselves and stating their needs (Elliott et al., 2004; Greenberg, 2011).

Principles of Emotional Change

EFT therapists are guided by five principles of emotional change described below: *awareness, expression, regulation, reflection,* and *transformation* (Greenberg, 2011).

1) **Awareness**: Increasing awareness of emotions and their various components is the most fundamental goal of treatment in EFT (Elliott & Greenberg, 2017). Lieberman and colleagues (2007) note that naming a feeling in words helps reduce arousal in the emotion centre of the brain, also known as the amygdala—in other words, you have to "name it to tame it." Emotional awareness involves accepting emotions rather than avoiding them; it also involves consciously experiencing them in the moment rather than simply thinking or talking about them (Elliott & Greenberg, 2017). Becoming aware of and symbolizing core emotional experience into words provides access to both the adaptive information and the action tendency of the emotion, thereby enabling the pursuit of relevant goals.

2) **Expression**: Emotional expression is a unique aspect of emotional processing that predicts adjustment to a range of issues, such as interpersonal emotional injuries, trauma (Foa & Jaycox, 1999; Greenberg & Malcolm, 2002), and even unforeseen illnesses like breast cancer (Stanton et al., 2000). Expressing emotion in therapy does not involve the mere venting

of secondary emotions. Instead, the focus is on overcoming the avoidance of strongly experienced emotions and expressing previously inhibited primary responses (Greenberg & Safran, 1987; Greenberg, 2002). Greenberg, Auszra, and Herrmann (2007) found that the manner in which aroused emotions were expressed in EFT distinguished good from poor outcomes. They defined productive emotional expression as occurring when a client processes the emotion in a "contactful" way—that is, without either being stuck or being a passive victim of the emotion.

3) **Regulation**: Awareness and expression principles are useful when emotion is absent or overregulated; however, when emotional arousal is too high, emotions can no longer help with adaptive action (Pascual-Leone & Greenberg, 2007). Intense emotions that need down-regulation tend to be secondary emotions, such as panic or despair, or primary maladaptive emotions, such core shame or anxious insecurity (Elliott & Greenberg, 2017). EFT uses a range of methods for helping clients regulate these emotions. Soothing can be provided instinctually by clients themselves or from the therapist in the form of a safe and calming presence, empathic attunement, acceptance, and validation. Therapists promote clients' abilities to be compassionate to their painful emotional experiences. Emotion regulation processes may further involve identifying and avoiding triggers, identifying and labelling emotions, allowing and tolerating emotions, using physiological soothing techniques like abdominal breathing, distraction, increasing positive emotions, or enhancing resilience in the face of painful emotions (Elliott & Greenberg, 2017).

4) **Reflection**: Over and above symbolizing emotions into words, reflection on aroused emotion helps clients make sense of their experience and encourages its incorporation into their self-narratives (Angus & Greenberg, 2011; Goldman & Greenberg, 2015). In this process, the client's feelings, needs, thoughts, and goals are clarified and organized into coherent stories, and different parts of the self and their relationships are identified (Greenberg, 2010). The result of this reflection is deep, practical self-knowledge. Situations can be understood in novel ways and experiences can be reframed, leading to new views of self, others, and the world.

5) **Transformation**: In EFT, the most important mechanism for changing old, familiar, painful emotions is that of transforming them into another emotion, or *changing emotion with emotion* (Greenberg, 2010). Maladaptive emotions are not removed, nor are they merely lessened by the person feeling them; instead, other emotions are used to transform or undo them.

Research has demonstrated that meaningful positive experiences can undo the neurochemistry and physiology of negative experiences. Frederickson

(2001) found that positive emotions have the potential to loosen the hold of negative emotions on a person's mind by broadening the person's momentary thought-action repertoire. For instance, the experience of joy was shown to produce faster cardiovascular recovery from negative emotions than a more neutral experience. Additionally, resilient individuals have been found to cope with negative emotions by drawing on positive ones to undo them (Frederickson, Mancuso, Branigan, & Tugade, 2000).

Building on the notion that positive emotions can change negative ones, EFT theory proposes that maladaptive emotions can be transformed by dialectically opposing, adaptive emotions (Greenberg, 2002). For instance, changes in previously avoided painful emotions, such as core fear of abandonment, can be brought about by the activation of incompatible, adaptive experiences, such as empowering anger, sadness of grief, or self-compassion, which undo the old responses (Greenberg, 2010). Similarly, maladaptive shame can be transformed by accessing anger, sadness of grief, self-compassion, pride, and self-worth (Greenberg, 2010). Moreover, hopelessness and helplessness can be transformed by adaptive anger. Once the alternate emotions have been accessed, these new emotional resources begin to undo the programming that previously determined the person's mode of processing. New emotional states enable the person to challenge their perceptions of self and others that are connected to maladaptive emotions (Greenberg, 2011).

Also contributing to emotional transformation is the interpersonal context in which therapy takes place (Greenberg, 2011). Lived interactions between client and therapist provide corrective emotional experiences (Alexander & French, 1946). For example, a client's feeling of maladaptive shame can be changed when, instead of the expected disgust or rejection, the client experiences acceptance and soothing from the therapist. Introducing new experiences into currently activated memories of past events has been found to lead to memory reconsolidation, as the new material becomes incorporated into past memories (Nadel & Bohbot, 2001). This in turn facilitates the experience of new adult understanding and promotes more adaptive socioemotional responses.

Three Phases of Therapy

Emotion-Focused Therapy can be broken down into *three major phases* (Greenberg, 2002, 2011; Greenberg & Watson, 2006). The first phase of *bonding and awareness* is followed by the middle phase of *evoking and exploring*, before the final phase of *emotional transformation*. The focus of the first phase is to establish a positive therapeutic bond between client and therapist while increasing the client's emotional awareness. The therapist communicates the Rogerian core conditions of empathy, congruence, and unconditional positive regard (Rogers, 1957). In addition, the therapist is fully present and highly attuned to the client's moment-by-moment emotional experience (Greenberg, 2011). The therapist's reflections of the client's experience encourage an inward focus on the client's lived emotions, including physical sensations and feeling states. A rationale for working with emotions is established.

In the second phase of evoking and exploring, the therapist facilitates the experiencing and exploration of underlying painful emotions (Greenberg, 2011). The process of arriving at an emotional response can be best enabled experientially, such as by having the client enact the part of the self that evokes the emotional response. Blocks to emotional experiencing are also identified and worked through.

Once the client's core maladaptive emotion schemes are activated, a window of opportunity is created for the transformation that characterizes the third and final stage of EFT (McGuinty et al., 2015). With the lived emotional experience now "open," the client can generate an alternative adaptive emotional response (e.g., self-soothing, empowered anger, sadness of grief, etc.), which can be used as a self-healing resource (Greenberg, 2011). The therapist's role is to validate the client's new feelings and corresponding needs. As this new emotional experience is strengthened over time, a natural action tendency associated with the emotion becomes activated (e.g., assertive limit-setting, or self-care and self-compassion) and eventually becomes incorporated into the client's narrative (Greenberg & Angus, 2004; Frederickson, Mancuso, Branigan, & Tugade, 2000; Tugade & Fredrickson, 2004, 2007).

Markers and Interventions

A defining feature of EFT is that interventions are *marker guided and process directive*. Certain in-session client states are viewed as *markers* of underlying affective-cognitive processing problems. These markers inform the therapist's choice of intervention, or *task*, along with the client's readiness to work on a given problem (Greenberg, 2010; Greenberg et al., 1993). Models of the key components involved in resolving these problems have been developed and empirically validated (e.g., see Elliott et al., 2004; Greenberg, 2010; Greenberg et al., 1993; Rice & Greenberg, 1984). Six main markers and their accompanying interventions are described below.

1. *Problematic Reaction Point*

    Marker: A marker for a problematic reaction is observed when the client expresses puzzlement about their emotional or behavioural response to a situation. For example, a client might say, "On the way home from work last night, I felt so down and depressed. I'm not sure why I was feeling that way."

    Task: Problematic reactions are addressed through *systematic evocative unfolding* (Rice & Saperia, 1984). In a slow and deliberate manner, the therapist helps the client bring problematic scenes alive in the session with the use of concrete, colourful, and expressive language (Elliott et al., 2004). The therapist uses evocative reflections and questions to bring the scene alive and heighten the client's emotional response (Watson & Rennie, 1994). The goal is to arrive at the implicit meaning of the situation that makes sense of the reaction (Greenberg et al., 1993). Resolution involves the client gaining awareness of their personal style or characteristic way of responding to certain stimuli (Watson & Greenberg, 1996).

2. Unclear Felt Sense

Marker: An unclear felt sense refers to the client being on the surface of a particular experience and unable to put the experience into words. The client also communicates distress or disturbance due to the experience (Greenberg et al., 1993). For instance, the client reports, "Something about this doesn't feel right, but I don't know what it is. It's really been bugging me."

Task: An unclear felt sense calls for *focusing* (Gendlin, 1981, 1996; Cornell, 1996; Leijssen, 1998), in which the therapist guides the client to approach the embodied aspects of their experience (e.g., internal physical sensations, images) with curiosity. Through a series of exploratory questions from the therapist, the client is eventually able to accurately describe the experience, which can lead to a "feeling shift" (Elliott et al., 2004). The feeling shift informs the creation of new meaning, which is carried forward as the client begins to explore wider connections and related issues, sometimes preparing to take new action (Elliott et al., 2004).

3. Conflict or Self-Critical Split

Marker: In conflict splits, there is usually one aspect of the self that is critical of or coercive toward another aspect (Elliott et al., 2004). There may be verbal statements of shame, such as "I feel like a failure," or self-criticism, such as "I should be further along in my career by now." There may also be a verbal statement from the client indicating that there are two aspects of the self that are in opposition, with accompanying verbal and non-verbal indicators of struggle and coercion. For instance, a client might say, "Part of me wants to leave my marriage, but another part feels like that's a bad idea."

Task: Two-chair dialogue is beneficial for resolving conflicts between two parts of the self, or when one part of the self dominates over another part that is disowned or disclaimed (Elliott et al., 2004; Greenberg, 1979; Greenberg & Dompiere, 1981; Greenberg & Rice, 1981; Greenberg & Webster, 1982). The two-chair task is set up by having two chairs facing each other, so as to distinguish between the two parts in opposition (Elliott et al., 2004). The parts are enacted by the client and put into live contact by dialoguing with each other. Thoughts, feelings, and needs within each part are explored and communicated (Greenberg, 2010). Resolution of the conflict split involves a softening of the critical voice, which sometimes consists of negotiation between the two parts (Elliott et al., 2004). Rather than conflict or coercion, there is integration between the two sides, along with self-acceptance.

4. *Self-Interruptive Split*

Marker: A self-interruptive split occurs when a client constricts the experience of a feeling or need and expresses distress as a result of the constriction, such as feeling squeezed, blocked, or stopped (Elliott et al., 2004; Greenberg, 2010). For example, when coached by the therapist to express anger toward their inner critic, the client states, "I can't. I feel so small and squished down, like I have no voice." Self-interruption usually serves the function of protecting the self from potential negative consequences of experiencing or expressing an emotion. Possible feared consequences may include: becoming overwhelmed by the emotion (e.g., "If I get angry I might lose control."); being unable to survive the emotion (e.g., "I feel like the pain is a black hole that will suck me in and I'll never be able to climb back out."); having one's self-image threatened (e.g., "Real men don't cry."); or being abandoned, rejected, or victimized by another (e.g., "I don't want to give him the satisfaction of knowing he's won.").

Task: Similar to conflict splits, self-interruption is addressed through *two-chair dialogue* (Greenberg, 2010). Each part of the self is enacted, and their respective thoughts, feelings, and needs are communicated through the dialogue. The self-interruption is resolved when the client is able to fully express, accept, and integrate the previously blocked experience.

5. *Unfinished Business*

Marker: With unfinished business, the client makes a statement that shows lingering unresolved feelings toward a significant other in a highly involved manner (Greenberg et al., 1993). They may blame, complain, or express hurt or longing in relation to the significant other. For example, a person might state that "I never forgave my father for what he did to me." Although the unresolved feelings are currently being experienced, there are signs that the expression of these feelings is currently being interrupted or restricted (Elliott et al., 2004). For instance, the client is unable to express anger or resentment toward the other and instead expresses resignation and hopelessness, which are secondary reactive emotions.

Task: The intervention for unfinished business is *empty-chair dialogue*. Instead of dialoguing with a critical or interruptive part of the self, the client dialogues with the imagined significant other in the second chair. Experiential contact with the second chair helps the client activate their internalized view of the other and corresponding emotional experience. It is important to note that the therapist's role is not to facilitate a rational debate between two people; rather, the client needs to be helped to arrive at and express their unresolved primary emotions and unmet needs to the other. Resolution occurs when the client feels worthwhile and is able to let go of the previously unfinished business (Elliott et al., 2004). This can be accomplished through one or more of the following ways: 1) holding the other accountable for the violation experienced, 2) increased understanding of the other or viewing the other as flawed, or 3) genuinely forgiving the other for the past violations.

6. Vulnerability

Marker: Vulnerability is a state in which the client feels intensely fragile, ashamed, or insecure and is reluctant to expose a vulnerable part of themselves to the therapist (Greenberg, 2010; Sharbanee, Goldman, & Greenberg, in press). Vulnerable refers to being open to being wounded or hurt. An example of a vulnerability marker is the client stating in a fragile-sounding voice, "I feel like I'm finished. I can't carry on," or "I feel so separate from the human race."

Task: The intervention for vulnerability is affirming empathic validation (Elliott et al., 2004; Greenberg et al., 1993; Sharbanee et al., in press). In this task, the therapist helps the client gradually deepen their contact with the vulnerable aspect of their experience in a highly attuned and empathic manner. The therapist's responses reflect the client's experience and mirror how the client describes their experience (e.g., the client's vocal quality). The therapist's responses serve the function of soothing the pain and communicating that the client's pain is seen and valid. With this support from the therapist, the client's intrinsic tendencies toward growth and hope are eventually accessed and the client is left with a stronger self-organization and a decreased feeling of isolation.

With the advancement of research in EFT, a number of additional markers and interventions have been added to the original six, some of which are: trauma and narrative retelling, alliance repair at ruptures, self-compassion at markers of self-contempt, self-soothing at anxious dependence, and meaning making at markers of emotional high distress (Elliott et al., 2004; Greenberg, 2010, 2011; Greenberg & Watson, 2006).

EFT in Practice: A Case Example

Lidia,[1] a single mother, participated in an Emotion Focused Family Therapy parenting group in order to learn strategies to help with parenting her 17-year-old daughter, Deidre. Their relationship was strained and marked by frequent conflicts that resulted in yelling by both parties, followed by Deidre storming off to her room and refusing to speak to her mother for several days at a time. Lidia feared that some of Deidre's friends were a bad influence on her and felt the need to protect her by restricting her social activities and by encouraging her to focus on her schoolwork and extra-curriculars. Deidre often accused her mother of not understanding her, being over-controlling, and being unfair. This hurt Lidia, as she loved Deidre and only wanted what was best for her daughter. However, no matter how hard Lidia tried to protect her daughter, Deidre became increasingly rebellious, sometimes sneaking out of the house and returning home drunk in the middle of the night.

Over the course of the parenting group, Lidia became aware of how her own emotional responses to her daughter's behaviour contributed to issues in their relationship dynamic. In particular, she noticed how her fear of Deidre throwing away her future made her more stern and quick to lose her temper. In light of this realization, she also began participating in individual Emotion-Focused Therapy. Once Lidia developed a trusting relationship with her therapist, they began to empathically explore her fear of failure as a parent.

Lidia's therapist identified a marker of a critical split between the part of her that is critical of her performance as a mother and the adaptive part of her, commonly referred to as the "experiencing self," or the "experiencer." This prompted the therapist to initiate two-chair work, which started with Lidia enacting her inner critic in the second chair, as in the dialogue below.

Therapist: From what you're saying, it sounds like there's a part of you that is very hard on yourself as a parent.

Lidia: I guess that's true.

Therapist: (in a gentle tone) Could we try something that I think could be helpful here?

Lidia: Okay.

Therapist: (pointing to another chair in the room) Try sitting in this chair over here.

[Therapist places a chair directly across from the Lidia. Lidia moves to the second chair, or "critic chair."]

Therapist: I wonder if, in this chair, you can be the part of yourself that criticizes your parenting. Can you speak from that voice inside you and criticize Lidia as a parent?

Lidia: (as critic speaking to experiencer) Okay... Um... You've let the ball drop. How could you let her behaviour get to this point? She is out of control and you need to get a better grip on her.

Therapist: What should she do to get a better grip?

Lidia: (as critic to experiencer) You should come down hard on Deidre when she disobeys and remind her that you're the boss while she lives under your roof. You can't let her get away with things and do whatever she wants. You know what's best for her. Protect her from her friends who are a bad influence and don't let her go out with them. Keep her from going out on weekends so she can study instead. She can't lose her focus on her future. You know what's best for her—don't let her make her own decisions. Be stricter. Be firmer.

Therapist: Uhuh ... She should be stricter and firmer. What could happen if she's not?

Lidia: (as critic to experiencer) Deidre will fail at school and she won't receive the grades she needs to get a scholarship for medical school. She could end up in a terrible job, living pay cheque to pay cheque like I do. She'll keep drinking late at night and eventually turn to drugs. She won't do well in life and nobody will respect her. You will have failed her.

Therapist: You're worried Deidre could fail at life if Lidia loses her grip and that means she will have failed her as a mother. (pointing at experiencing chair) What would happen to Lidia then?

Lidia: (as critic to experiencer) You would feel like hell. You'd know it was your fault for being a bad mother. It would mean you're a loser. She's already headed down that road. You're not doing well as a mother right now. You're already failing. (pause) You're a failure.

In the dialogue above, Lidia was able to experience herself as an agent of her own self-criticism. During this task, the critic revealed herself to be a worrier who feared the worst and warned Lidia to be vigilant and maintain tighter control over her daughter, so as to protect herself from imagined catastrophes and other negative outcomes (for more information on working with anxious processes in EFT, refer to Watson & Greenberg, 2017). Since this anxious process was conceptualized as a secondary reaction, the therapist guided Lidia to focus on her most feared outcome (failure) and, in turn, deepen her self-criticism. Subsequently, Lidia was invited to respond to her harsh and domineering critic from the experiencing chair.

Therapist: Now come switch chairs and be the other part.
[Lidia changes chairs.]

Therapist: What happens inside when she [the critic] says that you're not doing well as a mother?

Lidia: (as experiencer) (crying) I feel awful. I keep trying to do my best but it's not good enough. I feel like a failure.

Therapist: (in empathic tone) Uhuh ... You're left feeling so ashamed. What does that do to you to hear this voice always whispering over your shoulder, telling you that you aren't doing good enough?
Lidia: (as experiencer) It's exhausting, demoralizing. It undermines my confidence as a mother. I feel crippled.
Therapist: (in empathic tone) Right, the pressure is crippling. It's too much.

By having Lidia respond to her critic as the experiencer, she was able to articulate the emotional impact of the criticism. Her underlying primary maladaptive emotion of shame (feeling like a failure) was expressed. All the while, the therapist used empathy to deepen Lidia's experience of her shame and to convey a supportive presence. Subsequently, the therapist facilitated the identification of Lidia's needs associated with her primary emotion of shame:

Therapist: It really weighs down on you. What do you need from this part then? (points to critic chair)
Lidia: (as experiencer) I need her to understand how hard I'm trying.
Therapist: Yes, you need her to understand how hard you're trying. Tell her. (points to critic chair)
Lidia: (as experiencer to critic) I need you to acknowledge my efforts. To encourage me, instead of putting me down.
Therapist: Yes, you need her to be less critical and more supportive.
Lidia: (as experiencer) I almost just want to tell her to get lost (laughing and gesturing with her hands as though she is pushing the critic away).
Therapist: (in an encouraging tone) Yes, tell her to back off!
Lidia: (as experiencer to critic) Back off.
Therapist: Again.
Lidia: (as experiencer to critic) (in a more assertive tone) Back off!

In expressing her need for support and acceptance to her critic, Lidia's anger, a dialectically opposing adaptive emotion, began to emerge. The therapist was attuned to the way she expressed this emotion and recognized her laughter as a sign of discomfort with anger. The therapist responded by reinforcing and amplifying Lidia's subdominant adaptive anger, which served to set healthier boundaries with her critic. Afterwards, the therapist had Lidia return to the critic chair to respond to the experiencer:

Therapist: Now come switch back again.
 [Lidia changes chairs.]
Therapist: What happens for you when you hear Lidia saying that?
Lidia: (as critic to experiencer) I see how hard this is for you and I'm sorry that I'm not more supportive a lot of the time. But I feel like I can't trust that you will be a good mother without me. If

	you relax then bad things will happen. (points finger at experiencing chair) I am doing this for your own good.
Therapist:	Whose voice is that? Who has played that role in your life?
Lidia:	(as critic) That's definitely my mom.

It is not uncommon for a client's critic to reflect an internalized message from a significant other, such as a parent. Once Lidia identified her critic as the voice of her mother, the therapist recognized this as a marker of unfinished business. Since the unfinished business was at the root of her critical split, intervening in this domain had the potential to lead to change at the deepest level. Accordingly, the therapist initiated empty-chair dialogue between Lidia and her mother. To start, the therapist instructed Lidia to enact her mother's critical messages, so as to evoke her presence:

Therapist:	Can you be that part of your mom? How does your mom say that to you?
Lidia:	(as mother to experiencer) You have to be the best. Nobody will respect you if you're second best. Work harder than everyone else. Don't let them beat you. There's no time to stop and relax. Keep working while everyone else is resting.
Therapist:	Right, that's the message. That you can't stop, can't let your guard down. Keep working harder. Be the best. What would happen if she doesn't listen to you?
Lidia:	(as mother to experiencer) You'll amount to nothing. You will be a failure and I will be a failure as your mother. We don't have losers in this family, only winners.
Therapist:	Right, don't be a loser. That's the message.
Lidia:	(as mother to experiencer) You're not where you wanted to be by now in your career. Your wife left you. You've made poor choices. I'm very disappointed in you. And now with your daughter, you're setting her up for going down the same path.

After Lidia enacted her critical mother, the therapist invited her to switch chairs so that she could respond to her mother from the experiencing chair:

Therapist:	Come sit over here now.
	[Lidia changes chairs.]
Therapist:	What is it like to hear your mother say those things?
Lidia:	(as experiencer) It hurts (sobbing).
Therapist:	Uhuh, it hurts.
Lidia:	(as experiencer) I can never be good enough for you.
Therapist:	She leaves you feeling not good enough.
Lidia:	(as experiencer) And also so afraid. Always so full of anxiety.
Therapist:	Yeah, really afraid of . . .
Lidia:	(as experiencer) Afraid of being a loser . . . It's awful.

Therapist:	(in empathic tone) Yes, it's awful.
Lidia:	(as experiencer to mother) (crying) Yeah, I try my best, but it's like that doesn't matter. You don't see that. You just run through everything I do with a fine-toothed comb. Always pointing out where I come up short.
Therapist:	You're left feeling like you're not enough.
Lidia:	(as experiencer to mother) (crying) It's awful. Just awful.
Therapist:	(in empathic tone) Uhuh . . . Tell her about the most awful part about this.
Lidia:	(as experiencer to mother) I feel like garbage. I feel like dirt and I'm always afraid of messing up. (in an angry tone) I'm always afraid of disappointing you.
Therapist:	Tell her, 'It's unfair of you to put so much pressure on me.' Does that fit? Tell her.
Lidia:	(as experiencer) Yes, it *is* unfair. It's not what a mom is supposed to do.
Therapist:	Tell her what you resent.
Lidia:	(as experiencer) I resent you being on my back all the time.
Therapist:	What do you need instead?
Lidia:	(as experiencer) I need you to encourage and support me, rather than squish me down. I need you to help in a way that's actually helpful. I need you to be the one who believes in me when I'm having a hard time believing in myself. That's what moms are supposed to do. I need you by my side, not against me.
Therapist:	Yes, you really need that support and acceptance from your mom.
Lidia:	(as experiencer to mother) (in a more assertive tone) I need your support . . . (pauses and starts crying again) now, but also when I was just a little girl trying to do well in school and make you proud. I remember so much pressure from you my whole life.
Therapist:	(in empathic tone) So much pressure. It was so hard on you even as a little girl.
Lidia:	(as experiencer) (sobbing) It was so hard . . .

In the dialogue above, the therapist encouraged Lidia to express primary maladaptive shame in response to her mother's criticism. The therapist also tried to draw out Lidia's primary adaptive empowered anger, a dialectically opposing and subdominant emotion, as well as her unmet need for support and approval from her mother. Once Lidia could own these unmet needs and hold her mother accountable for not meeting them, she experienced sadness and grieved the mother she needed. In a later segment, Lidia responded to her expression of unmet needs as her mother:

Lidia:	(as mother to experiencer) I didn't mean to be hard on you or make you anxious. I just wanted to protect you from bad things happening. I wanted what I thought was best for you. My own

	parents raised me to live in fear of failing and I guess that's just the only way I knew how to be as a mom. I was scared and I put that on you when I didn't know what else to do.
Therapist:	What do you need her to know?
Lidia:	(as mother to experiencer) That I'm sorry (crying). I didn't mean to hurt you. I love you. You have so many good things going for you and I never really think to say them out loud and let you know. It's hard for me to say out loud that I'm proud of you.
Therapist:	What are some of those good things you're proud of her for?
Lidia:	(as mother to experiencer) I'm proud of you for the way that you are strong, determined, bright, and smart. And you're probably also a better mom to Deidre than I was to you.

Through the above enactment of her mother, Lidia experienced a shift in view of her mother as less powerful and as having problems of her own. More specifically, the experiential task helped her gain new insight that her mother's criticism was rooted in her own anxiety and self-criticism, and early experiences with her own parents. The enactment also enabled her to experience her mother meeting her unmet needs for approval and support. Even though this interaction did not actually occur between Lidia and her mother in real life, the experiential enactment led to a new lived experience that would become incorporated into Lidia's emotional memories or emotion schemes. In a later session, Lidia was eventually able to forgive her mother and let go:

Lidia:	(as experiencer) I know why my mom did what she did and I still love her.
Therapist:	Tell her about that.
Lidia:	(as experiencer to mother) Mom, I forgive you. I know why you did what you did. I love you . . . But I'm not going to wait for your approval anymore, or live in fear of not having it, because I can't keep living this way.

In working through her unfinished business with her mother, Lidia developed a better understanding of what underlay her own worry and self-criticism as a mother to Deidre, which in turn impacted her parenting. She recognized that her maladaptive shame and secondary anxiety were feelings that became reactivated in interactions with her daughter, and that they were not helpful in guiding her present-day decision-making. These insights were integrated into a revised narrative, one in which she was worthwhile and adequate as a mother. A new, more adaptive state of pride and self-compassion emerged, which was supported by her therapist, as seen here:

Lidia:	I'm doing my very best, trying so hard. Parenting is not easy. But I show up every day and give it my all. I really love my daughter so much.

Therapist: (in encouraging tone) Yes, you love her so much. She is so lucky to have you as a mother.

Lidia: If she doesn't get into medical school, that doesn't make her or me a failure.

Therapist: Yes, exactly.

Lidia: I imagine that just the way that I needed my mom to tell me she was proud of me and to encourage me, Deidre needs the same things from me. (tearful) Maybe she's going through the same thing I did with my mom.

Therapist: What's happening inside right now?

Lidia: Well, that makes me really sad thinking that she could be feeling the same way.

Therapist: It's sad for you to think that she could be feeling the same way because you care about her so much. What do you think she needs from you?

Lidia: I think I need to ease off if I want to help her and have a better relationship with her. I think that's going to be hard for me, because easing off makes me anxious. I don't want to go too far the other way and let her get herself into trouble. But maybe I could try having more of a balance of the two extremes.

Therapist: It sounds like you know inside what she needs and you want to give that to her.

Lidia: Yeah, I do. I can do this. I just have to remember to reassure myself when I get anxious and that feeling comes up again.

Therapist: Yes, exactly. That voice [critic/mother] is trying to help you, but instead it leaves you so scared and acting on fear. This voice that you are speaking from right now, this is what you know inside to be true.

Lidia: I'm going to listen to my own voice from now on. I can do this. Deidre and I are going to be okay.

Practical Strategies: What to Do

- Develop a positive therapeutic relationship, applying Rogerian conditions of empathy, positive regard, and congruence.
- Establish a rationale for working with emotions.
- Promote the client's awareness of and a welcoming stance toward their emotional experience. Help them put their emotions into words.
- Listen to the client's narrative and stay attuned to the client's moment-by-moment emotional processing.
- Assess whether the client's emotional responses are healthy versus unhealthy. Determine which emotions need to be more fully expressed and which need to be transformed.
- Balance empathy with process-direction. Facilitate experiential interventions to address markers of problematic processing.

- Follow the client's pain compass to arrive at their core underlying painful emotions.
- Validate the client's feelings and needs.
- Support the experiencing of new adaptive emotions and associated action tendencies.
- Help incorporate new emotional information into the client's narrative.

Note

1 Names and other identifying information have been changed.

References

Alexander, F., & French, T. M. (1946). *Psychoanalytic therapy*. New York: Ronald Press.

Angus, L., & Greenberg, L. (2011). *Working with narrative in Emotion-Focused Therapy*. Washington, DC: American Psychological Association.

Bechera, A., Damasio, H., Tranel, D., & Damasio, A. (1997). Deciding advantageously before knowing the advantageous strategy. *Science, 275*, 1293–1295.

Bortiz, T., Angus, L., Monette, G., Hollis-Walker, L., & Warwar, S. (2011). Narrative and emotion integration in psychotherapy: Investigating the relationship between autobiographical memory specificity and expressed emotional arousal in brief emotion-focused and client-centred treatment of depression. *Psychotherapy Research, 21*, 16–26.

Bowen, M. (1966). The use of family theory in clinical practice. *Comprehensive Psychiatry, 7*(5), 345–374.

Choi, B., Pos, A., & Magnusson, M. (2016). Emotional change process in resolving self-criticism during experiential treatment of depression. *Psychotherapy Research, 26*, 484–499.

Cornell, A. W. (1996). *The power of focusing: Finding your inner voice*. Oakland, CA: New Harbinger.

Damasio, A. (1994). *Descartes' error: Emotion, reason, and the human brain*. New York, NY: G.P. Putnam's Sons.

Damasio, A. (1999). *The feeling of what happens*. New York, NY: Harcourt-Brace.

Damasio, A. (2003). *Looking for Spinoza: Joy, sorrow, and the feeling brain*. Boston, MA: Mariner Books.

Elliott, R., & Greenberg, L. (2017). Humanistic-experiential psychotherapy in practice. In A. Consoli, L. Beutler, & B. Bongar (Eds.), *Comprehensive textbook of psychotherapy: Theory and practice* (pp. 106–120). New York, NY: Oxford University Press.

Elliott, R., Greenberg, L., & Lietaer, G. (2004). Research on experiential psychotherapy. In M. Lambert (Ed.), *Bergin and Garfield's handbook of psychotherapy and behavior change* (pp. 493–539). New York, NY: John Wiley & Sons.

Elliott, R., Watson, J., Goldman, R., & Greenberg, L. (2004). *Learning Emotion-Focused Therapy: The process-experiential approach to change*. Washington, DC: American Psychological Association.

Ellison, J., Greenberg, L., Goldman, R., & Angus, L. (2009). Maintenance of gains following experiential therapies for depression. *Journal of Consulting and Clinical Psychology, 77*, 103–112.

Foa, E., & Jaycox, L. (1999). Cognitive-behavioral theory and treatment of post-traumatic stress disorder. In D. Spiegel (Ed.), *Efficacy and cost-effectiveness of psychotherapy* (pp. 23–61). Washington, DC: American Psychiatric Publishing.

Forgas, J. (1995). Mood and judgments: The Affect Infusion Model (AIM). *Psychological Bulletin, 117*, 39–66.

Forgas, J. (2000). *Feeling and thinking.* Cambridge: Cambridge University Press.

Frankl, V. (1959). *Man's search for meaning.* Boston, MA: Beacon.

Frederickson, B. (2001). The role of positive emotions in positive psychology: The broaden-and-build theory of positive emotions. *American Psychologist, 56*, 218–226.

Frederickson, B., Mancuso, R., Branigan, C., & Tugade, M. (2000). The undoing effect of positive emotions. *Motivation and Emotion, 24*, 237–258.

Frijda, N. (1986). *The emotions: Studies in emotion and social interaction.* Cambridge: Cambridge University Press, ISBN: 0521316006, 9780521316002.

Gendlin, E. (1981). *Focusing.* New York, NY: Bantam.

Gendlin, E. (1996). *Focusing-oriented psychotherapy: A manual of the experiential method.* New York, NY: Guilford Press.

Goldman, R., & Greenberg, L. S. (2015). *Case formulation in Emotion-Focused Therapy: Co-creating clinical maps for change.* Washington, DC: American Psychological Association.

Goldman, R., Greenberg, L. S., & Angus, L. (2006). The effects of adding emotion-focused interventions to the client-centered relationship conditions in the treatment of depression. *Psychotherapy Research, 16*, 536–546.

Goldman, R., Greenberg, L. S., & Pos, A. (2005). Depth of emotional experience and outcome. *Psychotherapy Research, 15*, 248–260.

Greenberg, L. S. (1979). Resolving splits: The two-chair technique. *Psychotherapy: Theory, Research and Practice, 16*, 310–318.

Greenberg, L. S. (1986). Change process research. *Journal of Consulting and Clinical Psychology, 54*, 4–9.

Greenberg, L. S. (2002). *Emotion-Focused Therapy: Coaching clients to work through their feelings.* Washington, DC: American Psychological Association.

Greenberg, L. S. (2004). Emotion-Focused Therapy. *Clinical Psychology & Psychotherapy, 11*, 3–16. doi: 10.1002/cpp.388

Greenberg, L. S. (2010). Emotion-Focused Therapy: A clinical synthesis. *Focus, 8*, 1–11.

Greenberg, L. S. (2011). *Emotion-Focused Therapy.* Washington, DC: American Psychological Association.

Greenberg, L. S. (2012). Emotions, the great captains of our lives: Their role in the process of change in psychotherapy. *American Psychologist, 67*(8), 697–707. doi: 10.1037/a0029858

Greenberg, L. S., & Angus, L. (2004). The contributions of emotion processes to narrative change in psychotherapy: A dialectical constructivist approach. In L. Angus & J. McLeod (Eds.), *Handbook of narrative psychotherapy: Practice, theory, and research* (pp. 331–349). Thousand Oaks, CA: Sage Publications, Inc.

Greenberg, L. S., Auszra, L., & Herrmann, I. R. (2007). The relationship among emotional productivity, emotional arousal and outcome in experiential therapy of depression. *Psychotherapy Research, 17*, 482–493.

Greenberg, L. S., & Dompiere, L. (1981). Specific effects of Gestalt two-chair dialogue on intrapsychic conflict in counseling. *Journal of Counseling Psychology, 28*, 288–294.

Greenberg, L. S., & Goldman, R. (2007). Case formulation in Emotion-Focused Therapy. In T. Eells (Ed.), *Handbook of psychotherapy case formulation* (pp. 379–412). New York, NY: Guilford Press.

Greenberg, L. S., & Johnson, S. (1988). *Emotionally focused couples therapy.* New York, NY: Guilford Press.

Greenberg, L. S., & Malcolm, W. (2002). Resolving unfinished business: Relating process to outcome. *Journal of Consulting and Clinical Psychology, 70*, 406–416. http://dx.doi.org/10.1037/0022-006X.70.2.406

Greenberg, L. S., & Paivio, S. (1997). *Working with emotions in psychotherapy*. New York, NY: Guilford Press.

Greenberg, L. S., & Rice, L. (1981). The specific effects of a Gestalt intervention. *Psychotherapy: Theory, Research, and Practice, 18*, 31–37.

Greenberg, L. S., Rice, L., & Elliott, P. (1993). *Facilitating emotional change: The moment by moment process*. New York, NY: Guilford Press.

Greenberg, L. S., & Safran, J. D. (1987). *Emotion in psychotherapy: Affect, cognition, and the process of change*. New York, NY: Guilford Press.

Greenberg, L. S., Warwar, S., & Malcolm, W. (2008). Differential effects of Emotion Focused Therapy and psychoeducation in facilitating forgiveness and letting go of emotional injuries. *Journal of Counselling Psychology, 55*, 185–196.

Greenberg, L. S., & Watson, J. C. (1998). Experiential therapy of depression: Differential effects of client-centered relationship conditions and process experiential interventions. *Journal of Psychotherapy Research, 8*, 210–224.

Greenberg, L. S., & Watson, J. C. (2006). *Emotion-Focused Therapy of depression*. Washington, DC: American Psychological Association.

Greenberg, L. S., & Webster, M. (1982). Resolving decisional conflict by Gestalt two-chair dialogue: Relating process to outcome. *Journal of Counseling Psychology, 29*, 468–477.

Izard, C. E. (2002). Translating emotion theory and research into preventative interventions. *Psychological Bulletin, 128*, 796–824.

Johnson, S., Hunsley, J., Greenberg, L., & Schlindler, D. (1999). Emotionally focused couples therapy: status and challenges. *Clinical Psychology: Science and Practice, 6*, 67–79.

LeDoux, J. E. (1996). *The emotional brain: The mysterious underpinnings of emotional life*. New York, NY: Simon & Schuster.

Leijssen, M. (1998). Focusing: Interpersonal and intrapersonal conditions of growth. In E. Lambers & B. Thorne (Eds.), *Person-centered therapy: A European perspective* (pp. 131–158). Thousand Oaks, CA: Sage.

Lieberman, M. D., Eisenberger, N. I., Crockett, M. J., Tom, S., Pfeifer, J. H., & Way, B. M. (2007). Putting feelings into words: Affect labeling disrupts amygdala activity to affective stimuli. *Psychological Science, 18*, 421–428.

MacLeod, R., Elliott, R., & Rodgers, B. (2012). Process-experiential/Emotion-Focused Therapy for social anxiety: A hermeneutic single-case efficacy design study. *Psychotherapy Research, 22*, 67–81.

Malin, A., & Pos, A. (2015). The impact of early empathy on alliance building, emotional processing, and outcome during experiential treatment of depression. *Psychotherapy Research, 25*, 445–459.

May, R. (1977). *The meaning of anxiety*. New York, NY: Norton.

McGuinty, E., Nelson, J., Carlson, A., Crowther, E., Bednar, D., & Foroughe, M. (2015). Redefining outcome measurement: A model for brief psychotherapy. *Clinical Psychology & Psychotherapy*. doi: 10/1002/cpp.1953

Missirlian, T., Toukmanian, S., Warwar, S., & Greenberg, L. (2005). Emotional arousal, client perceptual processing, and the working alliance in experiential psychotherapy for depression. *Journal of Consulting and Clinical Psychology, 73*, 861–871.

Nadel, L., & Bohbot, V. (2001). Consolidation of memory. *Hippocampus, 11*, 56–60.

Oatley, K. (1992). *Best laid schemes*. Cambridge, UK: Cambridge University Press.

Paivio, S., & Greenberg, L. S. (1995). Resolving "unfinished business": Efficacy of experiential therapy using empty-chair dialogue. *Journal of Consulting and Clinical Psychology, 63*, 419–425.

Paivio, S., & Nieuwenhuis, J. (2001). Efficacy of emotion focused therapy for adult survivors of child abuse: A preliminary study. *Journal of Traumatic Stress, 14*, 115–133.

Paivio, S., & Pascual-Leone, A. (2010). *Emotion-Focused Therapy for complex trauma: An integrative approach.* Washington, DC: American Psychological Association.

Pascual-Leone, J. (1987). Organismic processes for neo-Piagetian theories: A dialectical causal account of cognitive development. *International Journal of Psychology, 22*(5–6), 531–570.

Pascual-Leone, J., & Greenberg, L. (2007). Emotional processing in experiential therapy: Why "the only way out is through." *Journal of Consulting and Clinical Psychology, 75*, 875–887.

Perls, F., Hefferline, R. F., & Goodman, P. (1951). *Gestalt therapy.* New York, NY: Dell Press.

Pos, A., Greenberg, L., Goldman, R., & Korman, L. (2003). Emotional processing during experiential treatment of depression. *Journal of Consulting and Clinical Psychology, 71*, 1007–1016.

Rice, L., & Greenberg, L. (Eds.) (1984). *Patterns of change: An intensive analysis of psychotherapeutic process.* New York, NY: Guilford Press.

Rice, L., & Saperia, E. (1984). Task analysis of the resolution of problematic reactions. In L. Rice & L. S. Greenberg (Eds.), *Patterns of change: Intensive analysis of psychotherapy process.* New York, NY: Guilford Press.

Robinson, A. L., Dolhanty, J., & Greenberg, L. S. (2015). Emotion Focused Family Therapy for eating disorders in children and adolescents. *Clinical Psychology & Psychotherapy, 22*, 75–82.

Robinson, A. L., Dolhanty, J., Stillar, A., Henderson, K., & Mayman, S. (2014). Emotion-Focused Family Therapy for eating disorders across the lifespan: A pilot study of a 2-day transdiagnostic intervention for parents. *Clinical Psychology & Psychotherapy, 23*, 14–23.

Rogers, C. (1957). The necessary and sufficient conditions of therapeutic personality change. *Journal of Consulting Psychology, 21*(2), 95–103.

Shahar, B., Bar-Kalifa, E., & Alon, E. (2017). Emotion-Focused Therapy for social anxiety disorder: Results from a multiple baseline study. *Journal of Consulting and Clinical Psychology, 85*, 238–249.

Sharbanee, J., Goldman, R., & Greenberg, L. (in press). Task analyses of emotional change. In L. Greenberg & R. Goldman (Eds.), *The clinical handbook of Emotion-Focused Therapy.* Washington, DC: American Psychological Association.

Stanton, A., Danoff-Burg, S., Cameron, C., Bishop, M., Collins, C., Kirk, S., . . . Twillman, R. (2000). Emotionally expressive coping predicts psychological and physical adjustment to breast cancer. *Journal of Consulting and Clinical Psychology, 68*, 875–882.

Tarba, L.R. (2015). Relating a model of resolution of arrested anger to outcome in Emotion-Focused Therapy of depression (Unpublished doctoral dissertation). York University, Toronto, Canada.

Tamietto, M., & de Gelder, B. (2010). Neural bases of the non-conscious perception of emotional signals. *Nature Reviews Neuroscience, 11*, 697–709.

Tomkins, S. (1962). *Affect imagery consciousness. Vol I: The positive affects.* New York, NY: Springer.

Tugade, M. M., & Fredrickson, B. L. (2004). Resilient individuals use positive emotions to bounce back from negative emotional experiences. *Journal of Personality and Social Psychology, 86*, 320–333.

Tugade, M. M., & Fredrickson, B. L. (2007). Regulation of positive emotions: emotion regulation strategies that promote resilience. *Journal of Happiness Studies, 8*(3), 311–333.

Watson, J. C., Gordon, L., Stermac, L., Kalogerakos, F., & Steckley, P. (2003). Comparing the effectiveness of process-experiential with cognitive-behavioral psychotherapy in the treatment of depression. *Journal of Consulting and Clinical Psychology, 71*, 773–781.

Watson, J. C., & Greenberg, L. S. (1996). Pathways to change in the psychotherapy of depression: Relating process to session change and outcome. *Psychotherapy: Theory, Research, Practice, and Training, 33*, 262–274.

Watson, J. C., & Greenberg, L. S. (2017). *Emotion-Focused Therapy for generalized anxiety*. Washington, DC: American Psychological Association.

Watson, J. C., & Rennie, D. (1994). Qualitative analysis of clients' subjective experience of significant moments during the exploration of problematic reactions. *Journal of Counseling Psychology, 41*, 500–509.

Wnuk, S. M., Greenberg, L., & Dolhanty, J. (2015). Emotion-focused group therapy for women with symptoms of bulimia nervosa. *Journal of Treatment and Prevention, 23*, 253–261.

Wong, K., & Pos, A. (2014). Interpersonal processes affecting early alliance formation in experiential therapy for depression. *Psychotherapy Research, 24*, 1–11.

Yalom, I. D. (1980). *Existential psychotherapy*. New York, NY: Basic Books.

2 Emotion-Focused Therapies for Children and Adolescents

Mirisse Foroughe

As an emotion-focused clinician working in a child and family clinic, it is not long before the thought of using emotion-focused approaches with children and adolescents comes to mind. This chapter outlines the process of attempting to apply EFT to the treatment of children and teens, and how the developments within this process ultimately led to involving caregivers in the treatment.

When we consider the central role of emotion and emotion regulation in the healthy psychological development of children and teens, the application of EFT to child and family mental health is a rather logical extension. Sue Johnson and colleagues have found the application of EFT[1] to children and families highly effective in their work (Johnson, 2013; Johnson & Wittenborn, 2012; Johnson, Maddeaux, & Blouin, 1998), the focus of which is fostering positive cycles of accessibility and responsiveness in the parent-child relationship. In Johnson's EFT for families, the therapist helps recognize attachment patterns and negative cycles within the family via dyadic, triadic, and family group sessions. By seeing the child individually, the therapeutic alliance is strengthened, and the child feels open to sharing things that she might not in front of her parents. The therapist then helps translate what the child is feeling to the parent in a way that allows cohesiveness and restoration of the family as a haven and a secure base (Johnson, 2013; Johnson, Maddeaux, & Blouin, 1998).

Although there are no known published studies of applying Greenberg's model of EFT to clinical practice with children, Robinson, Dolhanty, and Greenberg (2013) found that emotion-focused approaches were useful for adolescents with eating disorders (EDs) after successfully using EFT for adult eating disorders (Dolhanty & Greenberg, 2009). In another study, Diamond and colleagues (2016) compared individual EFT for young adults to parent-child Attachment Based Family Therapy (ABFT). In contrast to their expectations, the authors found that individual EFT was associated with significantly more productive emotional processing than parent-child ABFT. Both treatments led to significant and equivalent decreases in unresolved anger, state anger, attachment anxiety, and psychological symptoms. The only area in which ABFT was more helpful than EFT was decreasing attachment avoidance.

This is an important finding, as it demonstrates that while emotion-focused techniques can lead to greater emotional processing, it is actual parent and child interaction—as opposed to the imagined dialogue in chair work—that makes it more likely a child will seek out their parent.

While our clinic eventually combined the benefits of emotion-focused processing and therapist-supported parent-child interaction, our first attempts at using EFT in child treatment were in the context of individual therapy with a child or adolescent, where the format of the sessions (child seen alone) and the associated principles of confidentiality and autonomy in individual therapy precluded involving parents in a central way.

EFT in Individual Child Therapy

Using self-critical split work, some children as young as 9 years old can work through fear-based difficulties such as social anxiety, generalized anxiety, and specific fears. Many children are also able to begin processing anger and sadness and engage in a modified unfinished business sequence, enacting an experience between themselves and a significant caregiver in empty-chair work. In this sequence, some children seem able to work with their internal model of the hurtful/misattuned part of that caregiver. When children are asked to isolate and heighten the part of the parent that upsets them, many are able to do so, albeit sometimes with only slightly more laughter and awkwardness than adults display in similar chair work. Children can also be engaged in emotion-focused chair work for a current interpersonal conflict, such as a problematic relationship with a peer at school, bullying, or other social difficulties.

There are, however, important differences between EFT chair work with a child and with an adult. A child's attachment-related memories are obviously based on more recent experiences than an adult's. More importantly, the child will continue to form these attachment-related memories in their ongoing daily interactions with the primary caregivers. As a result, the emotional task is more akin to a "work in progress" than to "unfinished business."

When children engage in live emotion work, there are several interesting observations in contrast to EFT with adults. First, the core maladaptive emotions tend to arise very rapidly for children, and emotional memories are very close and accessible. The clinician needs to be ready to shift quickly into identifying and supporting the expression of the core maladaptive emotion, often within a few minutes of beginning the first attempt at UFB chair work. After core emotions are acknowledged, the resolution of the chair-work sequence can also occur rather quickly, and children can feel almost immediate relief from having painful or troubling feelings identified and validated in a single session.

In self-critic sequences, children can gain confidence and relief from "talking back" to their critic. After the self-critic sequences, many children spontaneously make comments about wanting to share their feelings with caregivers, but also express that it would not go well: "I wish I could talk to my mom like this, but she would freak right out,"; "You wanna come to my house and try explaining this to my parents?"; "Wow. So that's what it feels like when your feelings actually get validated. My parents would have shut me down two seconds into the conversation!" When these children engaged in an EFT Unfinished Business (UFB) task, very strong emotions became accessible. We will share the process of child emotion work with UFB in detail, especially when resolution does *not* occur within the intervention, because this can be very challenging to manage clinically. Importantly, it can also be the catalyst to using the real parent-child relationship in the therapeutic process.

Successful Task Resolution

For some children, expressed hurt is easily resolved with chair work. These children are able to imagine their parent softening in the "empty" chair and meeting their needs quite adequately, if not perfectly. The children display high levels of resilience and can imagine their parent being very supportive and responsive. They seem able to carry their newly constructed representation of the parent outside of the session into their lives. Often, only six to eight sessions of EFT chair work are required, and the child feels significant relief from problematic emotional reactions, particularly maladaptive fear.

Blast[2]

The second category comprises children expressing intense anger toward the imagined caregiver in chair work. These children strongly "blast" their imagined parent in the other chair and blame them for all that was unfair, painful, or difficult in their lives. They demonstrate open hostility toward the parent, reject the imagined parent's attempts at soothing or supporting them, and refuse any apologies or acknowledgements of their own pain. In their actual relationship with the parent outside of session, there is often tremendous tension and strife, and parents report oppositionality, rudeness, and defiance in their child. Other adults in their life may or may not have similar difficulties with the child.

Denial

The third category of children engage in "denial" when their imagined parent is placed in the empty chair. The most dominant emotion expressed in this group is guilt/shame in relation to their parent, followed by worry about that parent. The children cannot fully engage in the UFB task, and express clearly that they do not want to be a burden, or do not want to hurt their parent by sharing the strong emotions they are experiencing. Occasionally, their symptoms will improve, at least temporarily, simply by attending the therapeutic sessions and feeling like they are being heard and validated by another person. However, for most children in this category, symptoms will often return, sometimes in a form of a more pervasive symptom or clinical disorder. Common markers of this category are comments such as, "My parents are doing everything they can," "I don't want to put this on them," and, "My mom has been through enough," in justification for not being willing to express any negative emotions or share their hurt with the imagined parent. Often, there is a belief that their parents are not "strong enough" to handle what was going on for the child.

In some cases, children with this style show subtle signs of *wishing* that they could express their painful emotions to their parents, but these wishes are quickly shut down by their own processes. If the child displays this ambivalence, or openly refuses to express his or her negative emotion, the emotion-focused clinician can facilitate by identifying the conflict: "Okay, so there's this anger and then you talk yourself out of it, but the anger still stays, like you said, 'burning a hole in your stomach.' So, let's bring your mom/dad/other caregiver/bully from school in this chair and go to that anger." The child may still refuse or express reluctance, but the internal conflict, and the need to access their anger, has been named and targeted for future intervention. As well, some tips that might work to facilitate emotional expression include:

1) Moving the empty chair further back, so that the imagined parent or other is not so close to the child in the self-chair.
2) Putting the person in the empty chair in a "soundproof booth" and having the child express his or her feelings to the therapist, and then asking the child to share *just a small part* of what was expressed to the person in the empty chair when opening the "soundproof booth."
3) Processing the children's "block" to expressing the feeling by having them go into the empty chair and be the part of themselves that convinces them NOT to show the feeling, and to push it back down or hide it instead.
4) Using humour by encouraging the child to say, "My therapist is making me tell you that I'm mad, but I wasn't going to tell you," or having the child whisper or spell out the difficult statement rather than say it outright, etc.

Although these tips may be effective within the context of a strong therapeutic alliance, some children within the "denial" category of response still need a lot of time and practice before they can express their negative feelings, even to an "empty" chair. If the person in the empty chair is a caregiver or other family member, the clinician may consider holding separate sessions to prepare the other person to hear and validate the child's feelings, and begin making small changes in their current relationship with one another. These separated caregiver sessions are described in more detail later in this chapter.

Silence

Children in the fourth group are also unwilling to share their burdens with their parents, or to say very much at all when imagining a parent in the empty chair. Often, due to believing that their parents will not be able to handle their strong emotions, and shame at feeling any negative emotions and being a burden to their families, these children remain almost completely silent and shut down when faced with their imagined parents in the other chair. In debriefing with these children, they are able to express a strong fear of the potential fallout from sharing their feelings with family members. These children often need a longer course of therapy or to have their parents attend several sessions first, so that the parent can begin the process of becoming their child's emotion coach, and making it easier for their child to express emotions. It is important to keep in mind the child's fear of sharing feelings is not necessarily related to any particular parent behaviour. In other words, it is not necessarily what a parent did that caused a child to engage in emotional avoidance, but a combination of the child's own disposition, emotional style, family environment, and many other factors. Despite not being the cause of their child's tendency to avoid emotion, parents can support their child in gradually becoming less burdened and more able to process their emotions.

Of these three unresolved categories, the most challenging for us as clinicians can be the children who remain silent, because the emotions are guarded so strongly and are extremely difficult to access. In all categories, what the children seemed to need most was to *hold the parent responsible*. The children more likely to "blast" were stuck in this phase of blaming the parent, repeatedly using anger to cover more vulnerable emotions that would arise and be pushed down. The "denial" group blamed themselves instead and felt responsible for their parent's emotions. Children in the shutting down/silence group later revealed that they wanted to ask for their parents to take responsibility for meeting their needs, but they didn't believe the parent could or would, so it was easier to say nothing at all and avoid confronting the parent and risk being disappointed. What began to emerge in EFT sequences with children was that children needed their caregivers to be somehow involved in the process. The following excerpt is taken from an EFT session with a 14-year-old girl:

(Child in Self Chair)

Therapist: Okay, can we try something different? Picture your mom in the chair. What happens for you as you see her?

Tia: Nothing, I don't know, what do you mean? (laughs)

Therapist: Really try and picture your mom there ... how do you feel when you see her?

Tia: Mad, I guess.

Therapist: You feel angry with her, or ...?

Tia: Yeah, I mean obviously, because it's like why did you not even realize or ask yourself what I was going through while you were making all these good changes for you? Because I'm happy for you, you finally did it and you left dad and it wasn't the relationship you wanted, so now you have someone that treats you like you deserve. Okay, I get that. Everyone deserves that. But, like, what about my feelings? Did you ever stop to think how it's been for me?! (Begins to cry) No, you didn't. You didn't think of anyone but yourself. And the worst part is that you want me to just be so happy for your new life and the house and the stupid paint colours . . . I don't care! (Yelling) I liked our old house! I liked my old life! I didn't ask for it to be taken from me, it just was, and you made that decision.

Therapist: You had no say in losing things that were important to you . . . and you couldn't show Mom how much that hurt . . . or?

Tia: Yes, it hurt!

Therapist: You felt helpless . . . or sad . . .?

Tia: Both. So sad. I cried so much, and you didn't see, nobody knew it. You didn't see me cry because I wanted you to be happy. I wanted to be happy for you. But I needed you to also be sad for me, and you weren't.

Therapist: You needed Mom to see your sadness, to notice how much it hurt.

Tia: Yes! I needed that, anybody would need that, wouldn't they?

Therapist: Tell her . . . show Mom the hurt and tell her what you needed.

Tia: I needed you to come to my room, and just see how sad I was all those times. The whole time from when you guys announced it at dinner that night until the morning the movers came, every single night, I cried. I needed you to notice. And just be there for me like you have always been. It was like I suddenly lost you, just because you had him and you were so happy. I was losing my life, my house, my family and your support all at once . . . and . . . I just needed . . . (crying) . . . I needed you. I just needed you to help me know that I was okay and I wasn't going crazy.

Therapist: I needed you to help me with the pain so I didn't have to be alone in it.

Tia: So I could handle it and not start doing . . . forget it.

Therapist: Not start doing . . .

Tia: No, I'm not gonna say it. She's not here, it won't matter. She should be in that chair listening if I have to go through this to tell her how I feel!

Therapist: So part of you is saying 'I want you here now to see this sadness . . .'

Tia: Yeah. And she's not here, is she? It's me and this chair. I have a chair instead of a mother, this is so messed up!

The biggest challenge for the therapist here is deciding how to support the feelings and needs of children engaging in EFT. When Tia was supported to push through her anger and the primary sadness towards her mother was expressed, this sadness was validated in the therapeutic relationship, and to some degree this was helpful. However, unlike in adult EFT work, the adolescent's wish for their parent to be there instead of an empty chair is not an unattainable wish. Unless we believe that the parent is truly incapable of providing emotional support to their own child, and that belief is not simply based on our own fears about how to go about involving the parent in the therapy, why would we not try and support their parent in providing the validation and support that we are trying to provide on the parent's behalf?

Involving Caregivers With a Trauma History: Why and Why Not?

Often, parents and caregivers are on the periphery of the therapeutic process, whether they have a history of intrafamilial trauma or not. Parents with a history of trauma can feel even more guilty or afraid of becoming involved—very often feeling to blame for their child's mental health issues or too broken themselves to help "fix" their child. However, they may do practical things to support the child's therapy, such as: bringing the child or teen to sessions, paying for the therapy, making the appointments for them, and so on. While it may seem simple to just reach out to parents and invite them into the process, our "clinician blocks" can get in our way. These blocks include: worries about being rejected or blamed by parents, fears about speaking to a parent whom we may find intimidating, and sometimes anger or resentment towards a parent because of how strongly allied we are with the child and their unmet needs.

When we know that a caregiver has experienced intrafamilial trauma as a child, we may also be particularly reluctant to involve them in their child's therapy, or to ask them to assume the role of emotion coach for their child. Some of the parents' behaviours, such as escalating conflict or responding dismissively, can even remind us of upsetting things that our own parents did when we were children and can get in the way of our approaching them. While it can be quite challenging to work through these clinician blocks to involving parents in therapy, most parents respond quite positively when we reach out to them without judgement or trepidation. They may have wanted to be more involved in their child's therapy but had assumed, as many clinicians also do, that adolescents benefit from having "someone else" to talk to and that's where the healing happens. Parents may also feel helpless and ineffective, unsure of how to emotionally support their child when the child is going through difficult mental health issues. The parent's own lack of confidence can be indirectly reinforced in the process of taking their child to an expert therapist. As a therapist working primarily with children, it is also not always easy to feel confident working with their parents. Our lack of experience and confidence working with parents can play a role in our decision not to reach out to them, even when a child would benefit from having us facilitate the communication and emotional repair between parent and child.

Inviting Parents Into the Process Reduces the Risk and Burden for Children

As therapists working with children, we sometimes find ourselves helping them accept their parent's limitations and learn to adapt to these. From an EFFT framework, this would be a very last resort. When we decide to invite a parent into therapy, we are making the assumption that accepting a parent's limitations and finding alternative ways of coping may be adaptive, as it is for adult clients, but is *not the best and only option for a child*—especially a child with a living parent whom we can engage in therapy. If a child has felt repeatedly rejected by their parent, and is able to access assertive anger through the empty-chair dialogue with their parent, they may say to the imagined parent, "I deserve to be loved and you should love me." In EFT with adults, the resolution to this task might be acceptance of the parent's limitations, expression of empowered anger in empty chair work, or self-soothing and the grieving of not having their need met. *The resolution, for the adult, is to let go of that wish and find the love that they need within themselves*, not their original caregiver. In our experience, many children do not want to "let go" of the belief that their actual parent will, someday, be able to meet their needs. Even if they leave the therapy room feeling better, having provided themselves with appropriate soothing, reassurance, or other adaptive responses on behalf of their caregiver, the process affects change in only one part of the dyad. In effect, *the therapy may be changing the child's internal representation of the parent, but the real parent-child relationship is still actively re-creating that representation in the child's life on a daily basis.* The discrepancy between the child's optimal, imagined parent and their lived reality with that parent can itself become a source of significant pain and distress. By inviting the parent/caregiver into the session, we can reduce this discrepancy.

When we consider how dependent children and even young adults are on their parents for emotional, physical, and financial support, it becomes clear that we need to consider the parent's experience of the child as their child is going through therapy. For example, parents may become more dissatisfied with and withdraw support from their child if the therapeutic process seems to be increasing the child's emotionality. When EFT's tasks bring up intensely painful emotions, a child's expression of these feelings outside of the therapy session may lead parents to believe the child is "getting worse" or "behaving badly." Consequently, without an opportunity to work through these reactions, parents may withdraw their support of the child, or may pull them out of therapy.

Another benefit of involving parents in therapy is that it reduces the disparity that develops between the child and parent in the area of emotional processing. If the parent does not have support for their own emotional process, then the child's greater emotional awareness—gained through therapy—may negatively impact the parent-child relationship. For example, if a child's assertive anger towards the parent is adaptive, but the parent is not part of the therapeutic process, the child has two painful options: 1) express the justified anger to his or her unprepared parent and be met with a misattuned response, or 2) do not express the anger, further avoiding emotions and engaging in a form of role-reversal—the child is more worried about protecting the parent's emotions than his or her own.

When parents are involved in emotion-focused therapeutic process, they can be better prepared for their child's processing of emotion, as well as their own. This is because of another important risk of emotion work with children: they have a harder time keeping their therapeutic process private. Perhaps appropriately, given the importance of their relationship with the primary attachment figure, *children often cannot resist taking their new experience understanding in therapy and attempting to share it with their actual caregiver.* For example, the child may go home and announce, perhaps during a disagreement, "It's been your fault all along! I'm not the problem, it's just your bad parenting. That's what I figured out in therapy." Without any support in dealing with their child's newly formed ability to de-pathologize and rid themselves of blame, caregivers can feel intensely shamed and react with anger and defensiveness. This leaves the child even worse off than before, unable to find any validation or support for the intense emotions that have been brought to awareness in therapy.

Contrasting EFT and ABFT

As ABFT is an established therapeutic intervention involving separated and joint parent-child sessions, it is useful to consider what is similar and different between ABFT and Emotion-Focused Therapy with families. In ABFT, initial sessions serve to identify the patterns of attachment and negative cycles within the family (Diamond, Reis, Diamond, Siqueland, & Isaacs, 2002). Subsequently, differing family subsystems are identified and invited to individual sessions—each has the opportunity to speak about the role that they feel they play within the family. The child identified as the patient or client is seen alone, as well as possibly in dyadic and triadic sessions and family sessions. Intensive focus on the attachment relationship is most commonly seen within dyadic sessions, whereas individual sessions strengthen rapport between client and therapist, allowing the client to speak openly about subjects that may be too difficult to discuss in the presence of a family member. Treatment will end with a family session to discuss progress towards goals, and to ensure that any changes that have been made are integrated into the entire family system. The primary goal of ABFT is to help the child and parent identify, discuss, and work through past and current family traumas and conflicts that have strained their attachment bond and damaged mutual trust.

EFT and ABFT differ in their central techniques used to promote productive emotional processing. In order to achieve productive emotional processing, EFT therapists use a variety of interventions, including: empathic responses, focusing, and Gestalt-based techniques such as two-chair and empty-chair dialogue. In ABFT, productive emotional processing is not conceived of as an end in and of itself, but rather as a way to prepare the young adult to communicate previously unexpressed primary adaptive emotions and unmet attachment needs *directly* to his or her parents in conjoint therapy sessions (Diamond, Reis, Diamond, Siqueland, & Isaacs, 2002; Israel & Diamond, 2013; Wagner, Diamond, Levy, Russon, & Litster, 2016). Where ABFT uses corrective interpersonal emotional experiencing and emphasizes healing attachment bonds between the parent and child, EFT uses both the intrapsychic changing of emotion with a different emotion, as well as corrective interpersonal emotional experiences with the therapist and between individuals.

Many of the clinicians working within our team found ABFT and EFT worked powerfully together, allowing for deep emotional processing and the resolution of attachment anxiety in the parent-child relationship. EFFT brings together the focus on the parent-child relationship as well as emotion processing for the parent, which leads to emotion processing for the child, although the child's processing can happen within the context of the parent-child relationship and not necessarily within a clinical session. Indeed, many EFFT therapists do not work directly with the child at all, holding parent-only sessions or workshops. EFFT's emphasis on the parent taking "radical responsibility" for the child's emotional needs contrasts with ABFT, where both parent and child are involved and expected to work on improving their communication. We can think of EFFT as particularly helpful, then, in cases where children or teens refuse to be involved in treatment, or when parents need to process their own emotional "blind spots" or blocks in order to help move forward the treatment process.

EFT Kids Case Series—What We Learned

In our case series involving children aged 9 to 17, nearly 80% were able to engage in EFT with chair-work sequences to access, identify, clarify, and express emotion. Without parents actively involved in session, children often used chair work to imagine support from their primary caregiver. However, this "self-soothing" chair work (child acting as their own caregiver and responding in an emotionally attuned manner) did not provide most children with the relief that adult clients experience in successful individual EFT. Where adult clients would have usually experienced grief but been able to accept their parent's limitations, child clients seemed unable to stop needing their parents' support in this way. Some expressed hope that their parents could eventually respond in an attuned way to the feelings and needs that they had identified. Many others expressed anger that their parents would never be able to respond in the way that they needed them to.

It is significant to note that most children were not explicitly asking for their parents to become involved in their therapy. Even after realizing that the resolution to their emotional pain was related to the parent-child relationship, or that they were wishing for a different response from their parent, many children remained steadfast in their refusal to allow parental involvement in the treatment process. At the same time, they continued to lament the fact that their parent could not or would not be able to meet their needs, leading to an impasse in their therapeutic progress. Their distress was not understood as grief, and did not seem to soften into acceptance over time. It was a strong complaint, from a place of ongoing hurt and need, and it became apparent that involving the actual parents in therapy might be indicated despite the children's concerns about doing so.

EFT Kids and Caregivers Program

If it is important for young adults to have an actual dialogue with their parent to improve the attachment relationship with that parent—as Diamond and colleagues (2016) found and as our case studies also suggested—we can surmise that it will be even more important for children and adolescents to experience this dialogue. In other words, imagined dialogue with the parent (using chair work), although helpful for clarifying feelings, may not be enough for a child to resolve attachment avoidance and improve the lived relationship between parent and child. What we wanted to provide in our family clinic was the benefit of parent-child dialogue from ABFT together with the more productive emotion processing of EFT.

Preparing the Child for Parent Involvement

In order to prepare a child as much as possible for the dyadic or family session, the first step is helping them to feel safe and willing to allow the therapist to invite parents into the process. This is much easier to do if there have been no assurances of strictly individual therapy, cut off from any parent involvement. Otherwise, a new conversation about confidentiality and the treatment process can be started with the child, outlining the therapist's reasons for involving parents and how this will be done in order to protect the child from uncomfortable or emotionally activating experiences that might lead to greater conflict between parent and child. The therapist can suggest separated sessions to begin with, working up to joint sessions that are initially shorter in duration. Confidentiality needs to be negotiated carefully, so that children are assured that only the things they are ready to share will be shared, and that the therapist will support them in expressing their feelings to the parent.

When the joint session has been scheduled, it can be helpful to explore with the child all the possible reactions that the parent may have to the child's expression of hurt or unmet needs. Whether or not EFT chair work has been introduced, the child can be engaged to use chair work just to practice what they want to say to their parent and then to imagine their parent's response in three ways: "As you most wish they would respond," "As you most fear they might respond," and "The response that you think is most likely." The child can then be supported in processing their own emotional reaction to each of these scenarios, and how they would want to handle it if things were to go that way in the parent-child session.

This process can help determine how the clinician can best support the dyad, when it is okay to intervene and what is okay to share, and if the child would like to have some time at the end of the joint session in order to debrief individually. In some cases, through the course of this preparation, children decide that they might just have the conversation with their parent at home rather than wait for a joint session. Although we can point out that the joint session may feel more supportive and contained, if a child wants to talk with their parent at home in their own environment, as clinicians we can support this by doing everything possible to prepare the parent, even if there is only time for a telephone session. The goal of the parent session is to facilitate the parent's secondary emotions or core maladaptive emotions that may be triggered during the conversation with their child, and respond in a way that will be attuned to the child's needs.

Preparing the Caregiver

The first challenge of engaging parents is reaching out to them and securing a parent session if they were not expecting to be a central part of the treatment process. For some, it can take repeated phone calls or e-mails, expressing the clinician's empathy and understanding, and kindly but confidently emphasizing how important the parent is in this process. Other parents are eager to become involved and help in their child's treatment process, but this does not mean they feel at all prepared to handle their child's strong negative emotions, some of which may have arisen out of the child sessions and may be entirely new for the parent. Chapter 5 provides a thorough account of working through parent emotional blocks in support of a child's treatment, and this can be helpful in processing blocks ahead of the parent-child session. In addition, the following tips can be helpful for parent preparation sessions:

1) Hear their story first. Parents need a chance to tell us how difficult things have been for them, and this sharing of pain is an essential part of rapport-building, particularly for parents with a history of trauma. Trying to skip this and jump to the child's needs would not honour

the parent's own feelings and needs. We tell parents to "put the mask on yourself first, before you help your child." As clinicians, we need to put the focus on the parent first, briefly suspending our agenda of helping the child.

2) Validate the parent's story. Regardless of how unfair, critical, or self-focused the parent's feelings may seem, we cannot "argue" away their experience, and validating their feelings is a parallel process that will prepare the parent to validate their child's story, however unreasonable it may seem.

3) Provide direct, concrete coaching and skills training to parents to prepare them for listening to their child attentively, being able to tolerate negative emotions, responding in an attuned manner, and conveying with their nonverbal communication the same message that they will be giving in words: "I see why you are hurt and I take full responsibility for it."[3]

4) Prepare the parent for each of the possible reaction styles that children may present with: silence, blast, denial, etc. and have them actually practice how they would want to respond to their child.

5) Provide repeated opportunities for parents to process and practice in session, as well as assign brief "homework." This homework may include listing things that may be underlying their child's sadness or anger, or writing out an apology to the child for anything that was a source of emotional avoidance, such as the child's sadness after their parent's amicable divorce, or being the "good kid" because their sibling was so disruptive at home and parents could not handle any further demands.

6) Prepare parents for how it may initially feel as though you are taking "the child's side" in the dyadic session, and the parent may feel confused or betrayed if not prepared for that. Assure them that your entire goal for the session is to strengthen the parent-child relationship, and that this will start with hearing the child's "side" so that the parent can provide the emotional support or coaching that they've practiced.

When parents are prepared and supported, dyadic sessions can be a powerful opportunity to provide a corrective emotional experience for parent and child. Complete belief in the parent's ability to meet their child's emotional needs is the responsibility of the clinician, until the parent's confidence increases and they begin to experience a sense of competence and skill in responding to whatever needs their child presents with.

Parent-Child Dyadic or Family Session

When both the parent and child present for the therapy session, the therapist can still consider the option of separated "parts" of the session, meeting with a parent for a few minutes to connect and prepare, and with a child to check in about how they are feeling and offer support and reassurance if needed. The flexibility of the EFFT model allows for any combination of individuals to be present in the room, which lends itself practically to the booking of treatment sessions around busy and sometimes conflicting schedules as well as clinically to be able to see both parents, one parent alone, parent and child, and the entire family all in one session. These separated mini-interventions also provide more measured "dosing." It can be helpful to have a few minutes of exposure to expressing vulnerability in the presence of a parent, but entirely intolerable (and counter-indicated) to remain exposed for 45 minutes of discussion. For each dyad, the therapist needs to monitor the emotional climate of the room and each person moment-by-moment, ready to intervene as needed, and to end the dyadic portion if processing individually would be the better option at that time.

As a rule, separate processing is indicated when the parent is not providing a corrective emotional experience for the child, or is having difficulty processing their own emotions. Usually, the latter scenario is what causes the former—but some parents will be able to "push through" their own difficulty and focus on the child's needs in the moment, perhaps needing an opportunity to process with the therapist afterwards.

Case Example: Lisa

Lisa was a 16-year-old girl presenting for treatment after being diagnosed with Borderline Personality Disorder (BDP) as well as "risk of early psychosis" due to the presence of visual hallucinations. On a daily basis, Lisa experienced intense anxiety, panic attacks, feelings of intense anger (only expressed at home), school and performance anxiety, and social anxiety as well as instability in her social life. She was also struggling with issues of gender identity, sexuality, and existential depression, questioning the meaning of life and reliability of reality.

Because Lisa had already tried the first-line treatment for BPD, Dialectical Behaviour Therapy, for nearly two years, as well as pharmaceutical intervention with anti-depressants, anti-anxiety medications, and sleeping aids, a trial of applying emotion-focused approaches to her care was presented to the family as a stage-two treatment. The initial two phases of this treatment were informed by the approach outlined by Pos and Greenberg (2012), including stepwise approximations of the two-chair intervention in order to support the client with a BDP presentation in the process of experiencing and regulating emotion. Lisa and her family were engaged in five phases of treatment:

1) Phase One: Stabilization (Separated Parent and Child Sessions)
    a. Parents were seen for four sessions together, separately from Lisa, and four sessions each parent on their own. Parent sessions were EFFT-based, focusing on validating the caregiver burden that they

had experienced, de-blaming each parent, de-pathologizing Lisa, and galvanizing parents to do everything possible to repair the family relationships, support Lisa's emotional processing, and interrupt her symptoms. Lisa's father initially had a difficult time believing that his daughter's illness would ever improve, and expressed a high degree of self-blame for her condition. His feelings were addressed in individual parent sessions, implementing EFFT block work as well as the EFT unfinished business two-chair intervention.

b. Initially, Lisa had a very difficult time talking about relationships or feelings in session. She preferred to draw, had trouble finding words, would take very long breaks from the discussion and seem to be distracted or dissociating from the conversation, and would become highly emotionally activated when focusing techniques were implemented to bring attention to her emotions. Lisa would shift rapidly from intense anger to intense sadness and "shut down" emotionally, unable to talk for the remainder of the session. Using a combination of individual DBT-informed coping strategies, as well as gradual exposure to Emotion-Focused Therapy, Lisa's mood and behaviour in session began to stabilize over the course of eight sessions. She continued to present with a high level of instability at home and within the community, but she was able to process these experiences within the therapeutic session with increasing awareness, openness, and clarity. By the end of this phase, Lisa was motivated to better understand her own emotions and be free from the automatic and intense reactions, experiential and behavioural, that accompanied her feelings.

2) Phase Two: Accessing Core Maladaptive Feelings

Taking small steps and having sessions with just a few minutes of EFT within the clinical hour, Lisa was able to engage in more direct work with emotion, accessing core feelings of fear and sadness. She agreed to give up the option to draw instead of talk, was more responsive to questions and reflections (although she still required much more time to respond and worried that she had not found the right words) and began engaging in the two-chair intervention for self-critical splits, followed by unfinished business. Her activation was closely monitored, and de-activating strategies (pausing, humour, breathing, "light" conversation) were used to prevent Lisa from being flooded with more emotional activation than she could manage. Through this intervention, Lisa was able to access the intense fear that she used to feel when she heard her parents arguing. She recalled being terrified of her father's homecomings, and hiding in her bedroom closet with blankets over her head as her parents spoke. For Lisa, these arguments were experienced as enormous fights, during which her father was psychologically abusive and her mother was broken down. In UFB chair work, Lisa felt compassion for her younger self, how scared she was, how worried about her mother she was, and that the anger and anxiety she developed was a coping mechanism to keep the fear and sadness at bay.

3) Phase Three: Parent-Child Sessions (Separated and Joint)

In the joint sessions, Lisa was only engaged for about 10–15 minutes in order to "hear" her parent's apology, and their commitment to support her. Her mother apologized for placing so much of the burden on her young daughter, when Lisa was a "superfeeler" as a young child and could see that her mother was sad, had been crying, and felt stuck. Lisa's father apologized for the fear that his temper incited in Lisa, and how difficult it was for Lisa to express those feelings because it would have made her father angry at the time. Instead, she became angry—as her father said, "You couldn't beat me so you joined me, because that was the safest thing to do." He promised to change these patterns, not expose his daughter to conflict and strife because it is so intensely painful for her, and to create an atmosphere of safety in the home. Both parents also let go of the dream of having Lisa become an accountant or lawyer, and told her that she could study whatever she wants, or not study at all, and that her health and well-being were more important than anything else. In a follow-up session, Lisa expressed the freedom that she felt in hearing her parent's acknowledgements: "It was like, they got it. We all knew we couldn't really go back and change any of it, but my parents just getting me and telling me that I wasn't crazy or evil for feeling those feelings was like a huge weight off my shoulders. I literally felt lighter. I didn't have to carry around that pain anymore. And on top of that, they were gonna let me be me. What more can a kid ask for? Listen, they're not perfect, nobody's perfect, and they still have their moments . . . but they kept that promise that they made me. I can see them keeping me safe from going back to those places, and each day that I have that . . . like, peace of mind or peace . . . it makes me stronger. Now I can work on myself, and maybe one day I'll be able to handle people yelling and I'll be strong enough . . . I don't know. But at least I'm not falling apart anymore. I'm doing things. I have my art. And that's all because my parents acknowledged me. Validation is all I needed."

4) Phase Four: Maintenance

After the first three phases of treatment were complete, Lisa's symptoms had abated to the point where her psychiatrist removed her from the course of anti-psychotic medication, as well as removed the sleeping aids. Lisa then reduced the dosage of anti-depressants to the minimum dose prescribed, and maintained this for six months before attempting to come off the medication entirely over a summer. She remained symptom-free with respect to hallucinations, panic attacks, and intense emotional outbursts necessitating ER visits or hospitalization. She continued to experience moderate levels of anxiety, but was able to manage these and access support from her parents, as well as one therapy session per month for the balance of the year. After a full year since the beginning of Lisa's treatment, regular sessions were not needed except for booster sessions when she experienced a romantic break-up. At the time of this writing, Lisa is a student in her third year at a fine-arts post-secondary program, and has a steady part-time job teaching art to children.

Multi-Faceted Child and Family Treatment: The Umbrella Approach

To facilitate meaningful change in the mental health trajectory of a child or adolescent with complex needs, it is sometimes necessary—and most efficient—to take an "umbrella" approach to care. Under this umbrella, anything and everything is possible if it will serve the treatment goals. If parents are at odds or struggling to work together successfully on recovery tasks, co-parenting sessions are called for. If a parent is struggling to engage in the tasks of their child's treatment and recovery, individual parent sessions can take place in parallel to the child or family sessions. These parent sessions do not take the place of longer term trauma therapy—in fact, the parent work in this umbrella approach only goes as far as needed to successfully facilitate the child's treatment process. The focus is still on the child's mental health, and the clinician makes this clear to the parents. Many parents would not have sought out individual therapy for themselves, but are willing to work on anything that is getting in the way of their child's recovery. Of course, if a parent has a successful experience in the parent sessions, these sessions can sometimes be a prelude to traditional adult therapy. It is important for clinicians engaging parents in the child's treatment to have a plan of therapeutic support in place, with trauma-informed services for adults, in the case that a parent requires a timely referral.

Individual Parent Sessions

Meeting with each of Lisa's parents helped clarify the needs of each family member, as well as process the emotions being triggered in the couple relationship. Lisa's mother shared a history of being a "passive victim" throughout her life. She was angry with her husband for how his anger and rage had impacted the family, and she felt guilty for having allowed this to happen to her. She also experienced persistent anxiety and panic, which interfered with her parenting as well as her professional life as a teacher. She engaged in self-critical split two-chair work, building confidence in herself, feeling relief from anxiety through assertiveness anger as well as self-compassion, and realizing her need to be behave more assertively and less reactively in her relationships.

Lisa's father was suffering with intense self-blame, and shared a history of intrafamilial trauma including physical abuse at the hands of his parents and older brothers, and psychological abuse by his alcoholic father. He was also the youngest child in a family of seven children, and had grown up in extreme poverty. He had to literally fight his siblings in order to meet his own basic needs, including fighting for his meals. As the youngest and weakest child, he was often blamed for everything but helpless to stand up for himself out of fear of what his father or brothers would say or do. The shame that he felt as a child was overwhelming, and he had promised himself that nobody would ever put him down or discount him again. This need to defend himself and distrust others had been an enormous weight on his marriage, with family life strained by his frequent angry outbursts and displaced rage. As Lisa's father was initially reluctant to engage in counseling, and ashamed that his family even needed to reach out for help, the first step was using EFFT parent block chair work to access his internal desire to help his daughter's treatment, above all other needs or goals. After he was resolved to aid the treatment process, regardless of how difficult or shaming it might be, he was able to engage in EFT two-chair UFB to work through the emotions related to his early relationship with his parents.

Co-Parenting Sessions

It goes without saying that the child benefits from a positive image of both of their parents, and that a unified co-parenting team can move treatment forward much more efficiently and effectively than parents working against one another. In addition to seeing parents alone, co-parenting sessions can allow for the treatment plan to be developed with parents providing input and generating their own strategies. These sessions also provide a safe place to process negative emotions in regards to the parent's relationship or the treatment plan. A useful clinical tool that allows the clinician to assess the co-parenting dynamic, and bring it to the parent's awareness, is the McHale Co-Parenting Scale (McHale, 1997). This scale has a series of questions about how parents speak about each other to the child, treat one another in the presence of the child, and respond to each other's parenting. Co-parenting is an integral part of EFFT, whether parents are living in the same home, estranged, or actively engaged in a high conflict separation. The core goals of co-parenting from an emotion-focused lens are:

1) Identifying and processing the secondary emotions, and their underlying core maladaptive emotions, that are triggered within the parents' relationship and interfere with the goals of the child's treatment and recovery.
2) Supporting each parent to "build the other parent up" to promote forgiveness where necessary, and to provide the child with the best reflection of themselves, and of their caregivers, as they embark on a journey of repair and recovery.

The concept of co-parenting is paramount to the understanding and delivery of EFFT. Aside from the timeless wisdom that both caregivers need to work together, provide consistency, and serve the goals of the child's treatment, the reverence and respect within the parents' relationship is paramount. This truth holds whether the parents are together or separated. If one parent disparages the other, even in a subtle way, the message that the child receives is that part of the child is unworthy. To illustrate this, we can ask each parent to mentally add "*and that's half you*" at the end of any negative messaging (verbal or nonverbal) that they might be giving their child about the other caregiver. For example, having a parent imagine their child in the empty chair and then say to that child: "*Your mother is a liar, and that's half you*," is a powerful exercise in illustrating the messaging that the child might be receiving, and evoking the parent's desire to protect their child from negative messaging about a parent. We need to acknowledge that we are asking a lot of a parent to "build the other up" when they are going through one of the hardest times in their lives or have been embroiled in a battle with one another. Forgiving and supporting each other certainly has a cost, but the acrimony between them will be much more expensive in the long run, and it may cost their child's health and well-being.

The benefits of speaking highly of the other parent and assisting them even when (especially when) they are stuck in a "bad parenting" moment are reinforced in parent sessions through explicit coaching, anecdotes, and empty-chair work. Parents are encouraged to embrace and celebrate the inherent differences in one another and to build one another up in the eyes of the child. The greater the strain and conflict, the more focus there may need to be on co-parenting sessions.

EFFT as an Umbrella Treatment

While we can utilize EFFT as the main therapeutic approach for a child and family when the presenting concerns centre on relationships and emotion processing, there are many times when children and families presenting for treatment have developed entrenched coping strategies or clinical-level symptoms that need to be addressed with established interventions, such as exposure and response prevention for obsessive-compulsive disorder, trauma-focused cognitive behavioural therapy, or family-based treatment for eating disorders. Even within the context of a prescribed intervention program, such as a cognitive-behavioural therapy clinic in a hospital, there are ways to incorporate EFFT into the existing intervention. For example, EFFT can be used to increase the family's adherence to treatment, to strengthen parent-child and co-parent relationships, and to work through any obstacles to implementing treatment recommendations. By targeting caregiver self-efficacy, EFFT can serve as an overarching approach to working with families, empowering caregivers and supporting them until they are confident in their ability to support their child's full recovery. Under this "umbrella" of caregiver self-efficacy and emotion processing, many other symptom-reduction or coping-based approaches may be incorporated into the details of a treatment plan. The EFFT content itself may have a very small or very large role in treatment, but the overarching approach has an indirect impact, ensuring that parents are empowered to implement the treatment strategies that are being recommended.

The clinician can do as much as they need to do, until the family interaction normalizes and the parents take over the task of coaching their child through difficult emotions, preventing and interrupting symptoms or negative behaviours, and facilitating the child's return to their age/ability-appropriate trajectory of development. Viewed in this way, any intervention can be supported by the EFFT approach to engaging, empowering, and equipping parents.[4] (See Figure 2.1.)

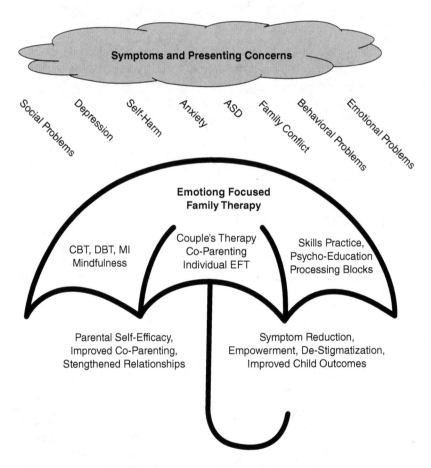

Figure 2.1 EFFT as an Umbrella Treatment

Summary

In initial trials of individual EFT with children, many of the child and adolescent participants were able to quickly access and express core maladaptive emotions using chair interventions. They also expressed negative emotions about their parent or caregiver, and these did not seem to follow the same process of acceptance, grieving, and resolution that occurs in EFT with adults. In some cases, the child's ability to access and express negative emotions increased tensions between parent and child, or resulted in lingering feelings of anger or sadness for the child. For example, children would often express unrelenting sadness or frustration about not being supported from their actual parent or caregiver in relation to the core emotional experience they had identified in their chair work. Other children would remain dismissive and interrupt themselves each time an unmet need or negative emotion was identified.

The structure of individual therapy for children and adolescents did not readily allow for the child's feelings and needs to be shared and processed within the context of their relationship with their parent(s). When some aspect of the parent-child relationship is not attuned to the child's needs, there is a crossroads presented for the clinician: to become the child's "substitute" attachment figure, utilizing the client-therapist relationship to offer validation of the child's feelings; or to support the primary attachment relationship between parent and child by working with each family member or dyad, as needed, so that the caregiver is able to respond to their own child's needs.

Notes

1 Johnson was a co-founder of EFT, along with Greenberg. Johnson's approach to EFT is called Emotionally Focused Therapy and is now distinct from Greenberg's Emotion-Focused Therapy in its theory as well as clinical application.
2 The categories of blast, denial, and silence are taken from EFFT's framework of a child's response to the parent's apology in the Relationship Repair task.
3 The emphasis on the parent taking full responsibility is a core feature of EFFT and explained fully in subsequent chapters.
4 This model is based on a similar model developed by Amanda Dyson, personal communication, Toronto, June 2017.

References

Diamond, G. M., Shahar, B., Sabo, D., & Tsvieli, N. (2016). Attachment-based family therapy and Emotion-Focused Therapy for unresolved anger: The role of productive emotional processing. *Psychotherapy, 53*(1), 34–44. doi:10.1037/pst0000025

Diamond, G. S., Reis, B. F., Diamond, G. M., Siqueland, L., & Isaacs, L. (2002). Attachment-based family therapy for depressed adolescents: A treatment development study. *Journal of the American Academy of Child & Adolescent Psychiatry, 41*(10), 1190–1196. doi:10.1097/00004583-200210000-00008

Dolhanty, J., & Greenberg, L. S. (2009). Emotion-Focused Therapy in a case of anorexia nervosa. *Clinical Psychology & Psychotherapy, 16*(4), 366–382. doi:10.1002/cpp.624

Israel, P., & Diamond, G. S. (2013). Feasibility of attachment based family therapy for depressed clinic-referred Norwegian adolescents. *Clinical Child Psychology and Psychiatry, 18*(3), 334–350. doi:10.1177/1359104512455811

Johnson, S. M. (2013). Exhilarating couple therapy: Singing to my soul—holding steady to my science—filling up my heart. In M. F. Hoyt (Ed.), *Therapist stories of inspiration, passion, and renewal: What's love got to do with it?* (pp. 146–157). New York, NY: Routledge/Taylor & Francis Group.

Johnson, S. M., Maddeaux, C., & Blouin, J. (1998). Emotionally focused family therapy for bulimia: Changing attachment patterns. *Psychotherapy: Theory, Research, Practice, Training, 35*(2), 238–247. doi:10.1037/h0087728

Johnson, S. M., & Wittenborn, A. K. (2012). New research findings on emotionally focused therapy: Introduction to special section. *Journal of Marital and Family Therapy, 38*, 18–22.

McHale, J. P. (1997). Overt and covert coparenting processes in the family. *Family Process, 36*(2), 183–201. doi:10.1111/j.1545-5300.1997.00183.x

Pos, A. E., & Greenberg, L. S. (2012). Organizing awareness and increasing emotion regulation: Revising chair work in Emotion-Focused Therapy for borderline personality disorder. *Journal of Personality Disorders, 26*(1), 84–107.

Robinson, A., Dolhanty, J., & Greenberg, L. (2013). Emotion-Focused Family Therapy for eating disorders in children and adolescents. *Clinical Psychology & Psychotherapy, 22*(1), 75–82.

Wagner, I., Diamond, G. S., Levy, S., Russon, J., & Litster, R. (2016). Attachment-based family therapy as an adjunct to family-based treatment for adolescent anorexia nervosa. *Australian and New Zealand Journal of Family Therapy, 37*(2), 207–227. doi:10.1002/anzf.1152

3 Development and Core Components of EFFT

Mirisse Foroughe, Joanne Dolhanty, Priyanjali Mithal, and Adèle Lafrance

The Development of Emotion Focused Family Therapy

EFFT was first developed as an adjunct to treatment for adolescents with eating disorders (EDs), and much of its philosophy, ingenuity, and the primacy placed on building caregiver efficacy can be understood in light of the urgent need to support a child's health and safety (Lafrance, Dolhanty, Stillar, Henderson, & Mayman, 2014). Although recent findings have revealed that supporting parents and caregivers benefits children with a range of clinical mental health difficulties, the urgency of parental engagement in a child's treatment process, and the necessity of emotion processing as an adaptive alternative to avoidant coping strategies, were both lessons learned from the treatment of EDs. In this chapter, the co-founders of EFFT share the story of this innovative model in their original application to adolescent eating disorders.

In their quest to improve treatment for a disorder with the highest mortality rate of any psychiatric illness, Lafrance and Dolhanty found inspiration in several sources, including the work of Gottman (1999) as well as Neufeld and Maté (2004). The story of the development of EFFT is a multi-faceted one, based on clinical theory, practice, and research from a number of therapeutic modalities: behaviour therapies, motivational interviewing (MI; Miller & Rollnick, 1991), Maudsley family-based treatment (Maudsley FBT; Lock & le Grange, 2005), The New Maudsley (Treasure, Smith, & Crane, 2007), and Emotion-Focused Therapy (EFT; Greenberg, 2004). While EFT was the final modality to be employed in the service of improving treatment effectiveness for adolescents with EDs, the co-founders agreed that the focus on emotion processing was the most instrumental part of their approach. The mechanism of changing emotion with emotion is at the heart of how EFFT works (Dolhanty & Greenberg, 2009), and it is applied to facilitate emotion processing for clinicians, caregivers, and children.

Before emotion work became part of EFFT, the founders were working in hospital settings with ED patients. Dr. Dolhanty was working with adults at Toronto General Hospital, while Dr. Lafrance was working with children and adolescents at Southlake Regional Health Center, north of Toronto. As the clinical outcome research was also showing at the time, the cognitive-behavioural therapy (CBT) focus of ED treatment programs at the time was leading to very poor results for patients with anorexia nervosa (AN), and randomized, controlled trials found no benefit of CBT as compared with other psychotherapies, leaving clinicians without any good options for their patients (Bulik, Berkman, Brownley, Sedway, & Lohr, 2007). Patients were often not able to engage in the program because their cognitive functioning itself was compromised as part of the secondary effects of the eating disorder. As well, many patients were so self-critical that there didn't seem to be any opposition to their very powerful, self-annihilating negative thoughts. Finally, they did not appear "motivated" to change these thoughts—they seemed to want to maintain the illness and/or believed that they did not deserve to get better. No amount of cognitive therapy was able to break through for the majority of these young women, and the illness would progress, relapse, and become chronic (Bodell and Keel, 2010).

Not satisfied with the outcomes from cognitive-behavioural therapy alone (Dolhanty, 2017), Dr. Dolhanty began implementing elements of motivational interviewing to enhance the motivation within the CBT treatment, and they began to see glimmers of hope: recovery rates began to improve. Moving forward, they added elements of individual EFT to address the need for increasing mastery over strong emotions. In the early 2000s in Toronto's hospital-based care, parents were becoming more involved in their child's treatment but their involvement was still peripheral. EFT for parent-child dyads was then added as a way to increase parental involvement and empowerment.

At the same time, Dr. Lafrance was seeing hope for adolescents with parents involved in family-based treatment, learning how to re-feed their children in the home environment and being told that, as parents, they needed to be the agents of change in their child's mental and physical health. However, not all parents responded to the call. Many seemed to shut down, back off, agree to take on the task but then fall short, expressing persistent self-doubt about their ability to help their child recover. These parents repeatedly expressed the belief that "experts" were needed to save their child, and that they, as parents, could not be the ones to bring their child back to health. Based on Dr. Greenberg's model of EFT, it is *not the thought or belief that comes first* (i.e., "My child needs an expert to save her") but the core maladaptive emotion (likely fear, shame, anger/resentment, or hopelessness/helplessness) that drives the parent's lack of efficacy in relation to the required tasks of recovery. It was necessary to work at the level of emotion in order to drive change in the attitudes and beliefs of the parent, and engage them fully in the treatment process.

As the evidence had repeatedly shown, treating the individual child, in the absence of parallel work on building capacity in the family to which they would return after refeeding, resulted in poor long-term outcomes for EDs (Lock & Gowers, 2005). A few observations convinced the co-founders that parents needed to have a more definite role in the emotion-focused treatment of mental illnesses, moving from a supportive to a central role in the emotional and behavioural recovery of their loved one. The first observation was that *the emotional "style" of the family appeared to have a significant impact on the individual's own emotional style.* Whether emotion was expressed in the family, whether it was expressed directly or indirectly or in a chaotic or measured manner, and whether emotion was dealt with openly or was avoided—all appeared related to the individual's own emotional style. The ability of a child to regulate or not regulate their emotional experience and expression, and the manner and degree to which adaptive or maladaptive regulation was used, closely paralleled the family's emotional functioning.

While similar emotional styles may be found amongst family members generally, this appeared to be especially important to pay attention to in the case of mental illness and life-saving treatment for EDs. This realization led to the persistent encouragement of caregiver involvement more urgently, explicitly, and centrally. This was not difficult to achieve for families of patients with EDs, as there was already a strikingly high degree of family contact, regardless of the age of the individual. Even the adult children usually lived at home, and even if they did not, even if married and with children, they were often in frequent contact with "home." Carers were usually involved in arranging appointments, driving to and from treatment, and the day-to-day routine of the affected individual's symptoms, lifestyle, and relationships. This ongoing closeness and contact between the family and the ill individual is not difficult to understand, given the highly impactful physiological, cognitive, and social sequelae of these illnesses. No surprise, therefore, that *affected individuals are highly engaged with their families regardless of their chronological age, and that families may become highly engaged in the trappings of the illness as well as in the efforts to deal with it.*

A third observation emerged from this pioneering work leading up to the development of EFFT. *Although carers were highly engaged in their loved one's mental illness, they were often ineffective in that role.* As Schmidt and Treasure (2006) noted, families often unknowingly "enable" the illness with a variety of unhelpful attitudes and behaviours. How could it be that these caring, engaged parents would actually work against their child's treatment and recovery?

It is certainly understandable that the life-threatening nature of severe mental illness breeds fear, desperation, and loss of previously adequate parenting skills and confidence. This confidence and ability to respond to the child's needs is sometimes replaced for families dealing with mental illness by an overwhelming sense of fear and the rationalization that "I would rather have a sick child than a dead one." Related to this was another observation: while parents were highly engaged in the child's life and their mental illness, they and their loved one presented as highly sceptical of having them participate in the actual treatment. The children were sceptical and resistant to the idea of involving their parents, and the parents were similarly hesitant, with both parent and child insisting that it would "go badly," and parents would feel to blame or blame themselves. These observations were documented in a research study, showing that carer fear and self-blame predicted low carer self-efficacy in supporting their loved one's recovery and parent's recovery-interfering behaviours (Stillar et al., 2016). In other words, when parents feel blameworthy, or other strong negative emotions, their caregiving confidence suffers and they tend to interfere with their child's recovery rather than facilitate it.

Core Components of Emotion Focused Family Therapy

If parent self-blame was interfering with a child's recovery, the founders of EFFT posited that parent self-efficacy would improve treatment outcomes. Seeking to eradicate caregiver blame and shame, and increase their confidence so that they can be effective helpers to their child in need, EFFT is a treatment approach rooted in a deep and unwavering belief in the healing power of caregivers (Lafrance Robinson, Dolhanty, & Greenberg, 2013). A transdiagnostic and lifespan model (any mental illness, any age), the aim of EFFT is to enhance the role of carers using an emotion-focused and skills-based approach, with four core domains:

Recovery Coaching

Carers are empowered to take on the tasks of providing support to their child and helping to interrupt symptoms. The recruitment of carers to support the behavioural recovery from the illness is not new, but to date has been associated primarily with family-based treatment in the treatment of children and adolescents (FBT: Lock & Le Grange, 2013), with the recent development of extending FBT specifically to young adults (Dimitropoulos et al., 2015). Although the nature and intensity of involvement may vary according to the child's developmental age, all carers in EFFT are coached to increase their involvement in their child's behavioural recovery. For example, parents are taught specific support strategies, as well as tools to support the interruption of problematic behaviours. This is done much as if they were nurses new to a psychiatric ward. Teaching carers these skills involves psychoeducation through lecture, discussion, and videos, as well as experiential coaching and learning via role-plays. During role-play, the clinician "sculpts" the parent's approach, for example, by shaping their choice of words, tone of voice, and body language. This approach is reflective of the EFFT principle that children are affected by the emotions that parents *convey*, rather than what they explicitly *say*.

Emotion Coaching

In order to lay the groundwork for Emotion Coaching, the EFFT clinician provides carers with information about the nature of emotion and the role of emotion and its avoidance in the onset and maintenance of their child's illness.

Emotion Basics

The emotion basics consist of four features central to emotion: that every emotion 1) has a bodily felt sense; 2) has a label; 3) has a need; and 4) has an associated action. Parents learn that the bodily felt sense of an emotion provides the guidepost to identifying and labelling what the emotion is, as there is a distinct feeling in the body for sadness as opposed to anger, fear, and shame. They learn the actions needed to meet emotional needs. Learning these basics enables the parent to manage their own emotions more effectively and to coach their loved one to do the same. The means of this transformation is Emotion Coaching.

Steps of Emotion Coaching

Carers learn the five steps of Emotion Coaching. These steps are derived from the steps of emotion processing in EFT (Greenberg, 2002; 2004) and influenced by Gottman's approach to Emotional Coaching (1997). His book *The Heart of Parenting: Raising an Emotionally Intelligent Child* educates parents on how to effectively aid in their child's ability to better understand and cope with their emotions. The EFFT clinician thinks of the parent's learning in the same way as they would a new psychotherapy student learning active listening techniques for the first time. The five steps of EFFT Emotion Coaching are 1) attend; 2) label; 3) validate; 4) identify and meet the need; and 5) problem-solve. Carers first learn to attend to their child's emotional experience by simply acknowledging its presence, as many parents are inclined to ignore displays of emotion out of fear of reinforcing them. Clinicians remind parents that attending to the emotion not only invites connection, it is also the first step in regulating the emotion so that it is more manageable. The second step in Emotion Coaching, that of naming the emotion, provides a label to a previously unnamed and unspecified emotion and continues the process of emotion regulation, and subsequently, of gaining competence with emotion.

The third step, validating the emotional experience, is the most important step in the process, yet the most difficult to master. The key to this step in the coaching process is for parents to be able to go from "but" to "because." For example, "I understand that you feel angry but you know I had no choice," becomes "I understand that you feel angry *because* you didn't want to have to eat your lunch in the car with me. I imagine you also feel embarrassed *because* none of your friends' moms come to the school."

The fourth step of Emotion Coaching is to identify and meet the emotional need. The EFFT clinician coaches the parent to respond to their child's sadness with soothing, and to anger with validation and support to set boundaries. In the early stages, the parent will be responding to the emotional needs of their child as though they were younger but using developmentally appropriate language.

With the fifth step, "problem-solving" or "fix it," parents often report that as they engage in the first four steps of the coaching, their child will often come to their own means of "solving the problem," or they will come to the realization that in fact there is no problem to be solved since the "problem" was really the experience of emotional pain. In some specific circumstances, however, such as in the case of bullying in children or unsafe relationships in adults, the carers must engage their loved one in problem-solving to address the situation practically.

These "Emotion Coaching" interventions are useful in many ways. First, as carers adopt this new way of relating to their child, the parent-child relationship will deepen, and the parent's efforts to support their child with the behavioural symptoms will be more effective and better received. Second, as the child reduces the frequency of her symptoms, her parent's emotional support will help her manage the flood of emotions that inevitably emerges in this stage of recovery. Finally, the over-arching goal of Emotion Coaching is to support carers as they support their child in "internalizing" the ability to later manage their emotions and self-regulate.

Relationship Repair

Relationship Repair is based on research on forgiveness in relationships (Greenberg, Warwar, & Malcom, 2008) and is a powerful intervention for caregivers and families. It can be especially relevant if the child or parent blames themselves or each other for the mental illness; if the relationship between parent and child is distant or strained, making it difficult for carers to take on an active role in treatment; or if the carers identify a pattern of emotion avoidance in the family that must be interrupted to support recovery. The EFFT clinician supports the parent to reflect on and identify any possible lived traumas, separations, conflicts, or even misunderstandings or misattunements that could have contributed to the child's avoidance of emotion and turned them away from seeking support[1] from the parent. In these instances, carers are coached to support the child with his or her pain first by using the steps of Emotion Coaching and then by expressing healthy accountability, via an apology, in response to "what their child lived through." One parent referred to this process as taking the chemotherapy herself to free her child from the cancer of self-blame. Some carers or even clinicians will ask: Why does it have to be anybody's fault when it is really nobody's? And the answer is that deep down most children will feel to blame and most parents will blame themselves. Relationship Repair is thus a process through which both parent and child can release themselves from maladaptive self-blame and shame, and be able to move forward. This step cannot be skipped.

Processing Emotional Blocks

There is growing awareness and recognition that the emotions of parents of individuals with mental illnesses interfere with caregiving efforts (Goddard et al., 2011; Kyriacou, Treasure, & Schmidt, 2008; Lafrance Robinson, Dolhanty, & Greenberg, 2013; Schmidt & Treasure, 2006; Treasure, Smith, & Crane, 2007). In fact, even though the primary aim of EFFT is to support and empower carers to adopt a primary role in their loved one's behavioural and emotional recovery, the over-arching target of the therapy is the attention paid to emotional "blocks" in carers. Parent blocks can appear "behaviourally" in a variety of ways, including refusal to become involved, denial, over-control, criticism, and accommodating and enabling behaviours. These behaviours are regarded as efforts to regulate the carer's own strong negative emotions, namely, fear, shame, helplessness, hopelessness, and resentment.

Parent Blocks

One of the ways that clinicians can help to process carer fear, shame, hopelessness, helplessness, and feelings of resentment is to use the steps of Emotion Coaching to validate the carer's experience, in the same manner that the clinician will teach the carer to validate those of the child. In some cases, we have observed that simply bringing into awareness and validating the impact that the carer's emotional blocks have on their ability to feel compassionately toward their child, to feel confident in themselves, and to be able to engage in the tasks of home-based treatment can free carers to follow the treatment protocol. Awareness, too, of their own history of unmet emotional needs and unresolved emotional pain can help to loosen the grip these can have, and subsequently allow the carer to attend to their child's emotional needs more effectively. Carers can complete self-assessment tools that help them to identify their emotional blocks.[2] They are also presented with the New Maudsley's Animal Models (Treasure, Schmidt, & Macdonald, 2009). The Animal Models illustrate common (and problematic) emotional and behavioural response patterns that carers engage in when caring for someone with a mental illness. Parents are taught to identify the animal best representing their emotion coping style, be it the transparency and "wobbliness" of the Jellyfish, the head in the sand of the Ostrich, with the aim of moving towards the calm and supportive warmth of the St. Bernard. In terms of caregiving style, they can identify as the Rhino charging in, or the Kangaroo with the loved one protected in their pouch, again with the aim of moving towards the ideal of the playful and nudging Dolphin as companion. These depictions provide a non-threatening way for parents to identify themselves and their partner, and to share their realizations with their loved one, providing a common language and de-pathologizing metaphors to address painful patterns that may have developed in response to stressors or go back several generations within a family.

Should these interventions fail to engage the carer effectively in the tasks, the EFFT clinician can work with the carer using an EFFT version of "chair-work" (inspired by self-interruptive split work in traditional EFT) to attend to and process the emotional blocks driving the therapy-interfering behaviours.[3] Such blocks may occur in parents feeling unable to engage in a behaviour to help their loved one, or in feeling unable to stop an unhelpful pattern. The example below illustrates an example of a parent feeling unable to help her daughter who is struggling with a mental illness that impedes her ability to engage with peers and friends.

SCRIPT OF PARENT BLOCK

Step 1. The parent begins in the "self" chair. The clinician and the parent work together to frame the block. In this example, the parent feels incapable of helping her young adult daughter engage socially in her first year of university.

Parent: It's better if I just leave her alone and let her manage it. There is nothing I can do, she has her own life now.

Step 2. Switch the parent to the "other" chair. Have the parent picture herself in the "self" chair and convince her "self" not to help her daughter with eating. Have her be specific about how it will be bad for *her* (the mother) if she does help. Have her tell the "self" what to do instead.

Clinician: Picture yourself in the chair facing you. Be the part of you that convinces you not to help her with her social isolation, to back off instead.

Parent: Okay, um ... don't do that, because you don't know what you are doing, and you're going to mess it up, and you're going to make things worse.

Clinician: Really scare yourself by telling yourself how badly it will go for your daughter.

Parent: She'll end up just pushing back and becoming more isolated, depressed, or even worse killing herself.

Clinician: And be specific by telling yourself how badly it will go for you if all of this happens.

Parent: She's going to hate you. And then you'll have really lost her. And if anything happens to her because you pushed her too hard, you will NEVER forgive yourself because you'll be the one who has done this to her. It will be your fault.

Clinician: Tell her (the imagined self) what to do instead of helping.

Parent: Don't push the agenda of 'moms can help with friends.' Just avoid it and steer clear of the whole thing. Let her handle it. She prefers to do things on her own anyway.

Step 3. Switch the parent to the "self" chair. Instruct the parent to picture her daughter in the other chair. Tell the parent to tell the child (who is being pictured in the other chair) that she (the mother) can't help her (the daughter). Instruct the parent to explain that her own (the mother's) fear that she will make things worse is too strong so she

Development and Core Components of EFFT 53

cannot help her daughter, and her daughter will need to deal with things on her own.

Clinician: Imagine Vanessa in the other chair. Tell her: 'It's not a good idea for me to help you. I can't help you. I'm too nervous about screwing up and being to blame if it goes badly.'

Parent: Vanessa, I'm really sorry but I just can't help you. I'm too scared to make it worse.

Step 4. Switch the parent to the "other" chair where she will "be" her daughter.

Clinician: Be Vanessa. Tell Mom what it's like to hear that.

Parent as daughter: (looks sad) Wow. I say that I don't want you involved because you get on my case but it's devastating to hear that—like, there's no hope. Actually it makes me mad that you can't find a way to support me and be there for me in a better way.

Clinician: As Vanessa, tell Mom what is underneath the anger.

Parent as daughter: I'm scared. I can't do this alone. And I do want you involved on some level. I just can't say that out loud. It's scary. I need you to be able to help me. I feel like you're the only one who really can. You're my mom. I need you. I need for one of us to not be scared.

Step 5. Switch the parent to the "self" chair and ask her to reflect on what it is like to hear that from her daughter—and what she now wants to do for her daughter instead.

Clinician: What's that like for you to hear? What do you want to do for Vanessa?

Parent: To clinician: Oh . . . I never think of it like that. I forget that she is my little girl and that she needs me. She puts up such a tough front. Vanessa—I am so sorry. I know that you need your mom. I am going to do this. I will get better at helping you. I won't let my fears get in the way.

Clinician: Like—'I'll figure it out?'

Parent: Yeah—I won't give up. I'll keep working with the team until we find the way.

Step 6. Switch the parent to the "other" chair where she responds as daughter.

Clinician: How does Vanessa respond?

Parent as daughter: It feels good. (She lets out a sigh) Nervous but good. I feel grateful. I really want things to be better and I need your help. Please believe in me. I need you to believe in me.

Step 7. Switch the parent to the "self" chair. Ask the parent to tell the clinician what it's like to hear this.

Clinician: What's it like to hear her say that?
Parent: It's touching. It's so easy to forget. Since she's had this illness she just appears not to care about me at all and not to want me in her life. And I believed her! That must have been so scary for her. It's hard to hear this but it does feel good to remember that she needs me.
Clinician: Can you tell her that? I forget . . .
Parent: Yeah—I'm sorry that I forget that. I've been so beside myself and so burned out by this thing. I do know that you need me. Wow—it feels good to find that part of me again. A bit scary too but good.

Clinician Blocks

Treatment is an emotional experience for the clinicians as well. In 2012, Thompson-Brenner, Satir, Franko, and Herzog conducted a literature review of clinician reactions to individuals with mental illnesses and found that negative reactions in regard to patients typically reflected frustration, hopelessness, lack of competence, and worry. Treatment resistance, ego-syntonicity, high relapse rates, worry about patient survival, emotional drain, lack of appropriate financial reimbursement, and extra hours spent working also contributed significantly to feelings of burnout reported by clinicians working with mental illness (Warren, Schafer, Crowley, & Olivardia, 2013).

Two theoretical models have recently emerged that identify clinician factors related to emotion that can interfere with treatment delivery. The Iatrogenic Maintenance Model (Treasure, Crane, McKnight, Buchanan, Wolfe, 2011) and the Clinician Drift Model (Waller, 2009) describe various ways that clinician emotion can interfere with treatment delivery. Clinician anxiety has been found to be related to lower levels of adherence to evidence-based practices in the treatment of both child and adolescent, and adult mental illness (Waller, Stringer, & Meyer, 2012). Lafrance Robinson and Kosmerly (2015) conducted a survey among child and adolescent clinicians to explore clinicians' perceptions of the negative influence of their own emotions on clinical decisions and practices in treatment. Whether they responded about themselves or their colleagues, decisions regarding the involvement of the family were perceived to be the most emotionally charged, in particular the involvement of a critical or dismissive parent.

In the context of EFFT, when faced with an emotionally charged session or decision, or when treatment is stuck, clinicians engage in "emotion-focused" supervision to identify and work through the emotional "blocks" that surface in therapy. For example, a clinician working with this approach may hesitate to enlist carers as recovery allies if the parent appears to be excessively hostile or in denial of the severity of the symptoms, both of which can be common reactions to the challenge that the mental illness presents to the family. Similarly, when a parent has a trauma history or is also suffering from an active mental illness, the clinician may rationalize that this parent is not capable of being part of their loved one's recovery. Every clinician, in fact, will present with the case of "What about the parent who . . .?": "What about the parent who has their own mental illness or addiction?", "What about the parent who has Borderline Personality Disorder?" Valid as all of these concerns are, the clinician can work productively with their own feelings about the situation to restore their empathy for the family's struggle, and open new pathways to working with carers as allies.

There are several modalities through which EFFT clinicians can engage in supervision around clinician blocks. They can engage in regular "talk" supervision to explore the emotions evoked in response to the work with a family. They can complete an emotion-focused self-assessment tool to help identify potential emotional blocks in administering the therapy. In addition, and similar to the structured "chair" tasks for the resolution of parent blocks, emotion-focused supervision can involve using EFFT chair work to process the clinician blocks. This could entail having the clinician begin with the self-interruption: "Don't involve this mom in the therapy."

SCRIPT OF A CLINICIAN BLOCK

> *Step 1.* The supervisee begins in the "self" chair. The supervisor and supervisee formulate the block. In this example, the supervisee hesitates to invite the adult client's mother to therapy.
>
> *Supervisee:* Julia's mother is very enabling. She makes it easy for Julia to hide out in her room and not engage in any social or familial activities. She's just going to make things worse.
>
> *Step 2.* Switch the supervisee to the "other" chair. Instruct her to picture her "self" in the empty chair. Instruct her to be the part of her that stops her from bringing the client's mother into session. Have her tell her "self" specifically how it would be bad for the client if she invited the parent to engage in her child's social recovery. Have her tell her "self" specifically how it would also be bad for her, the clinician.
>
> *Supervisor:* Picture yourself in the chair facing you. Be the part of you that stops you from bringing in Mom. Encourage 'her' (imagined self) to protect the child from the parent's involvement in treatment. Tell 'her' how it will go poorly for her (the clinician) as well.
>
> *Supervisee:* Don't let Julia's mother into the treatment. She is too soft. She will just enable her daughter and she will stop the therapy from moving forward. Julia does not need this on top of everything else she is working through. She's working way too hard. And

	you don't need to deal with the extra back-tracking. You're already drowning with this case.
Supervisor:	Tell her (the imagined self) what to do instead of bringing in the mom.
Supervisee:	Don't push the agenda of Mom's involvement. If Mom calls, let her know that it may not be the best time for her to join the therapy.

Step 3. Switch supervisee into the "self" chair: The supervisor instructs the supervisee to picture the child in the "other" chair. Have the supervisee tell the child that her parent can't help her—that, in fact, the parent may be damaging to her progress.

Supervisor:	Imagine Julia in the other chair. Tell her: I just don't believe that it's a good idea for your mom to be involved. She is not strong enough. I don't think she can be helpful to you. I don't think you can handle what's going on and I don't want to deal with it either.
Supervisee:	Julia, I'm really sorry but I just don't think your mom can help you. Uh, I really don't like saying that.

Step 4. Switch the supervisee to the "other" chair where the supervisee will respond as the client.

Supervisor:	Be Julia. Tell her [the supervisee] what it's like to hear that.
Supervisee as client:	Wow. I say that I don't want her to be involved because I don't think that she can handle it but it's devastating to hear that there is no hope. Actually, it makes me mad that you won't find a way to support her to be there for me in a better way.
Supervisor:	As Julia, what do you want her [the supervisee] to know?
Supervisee:	That I can't do this alone. And I do want my mom involved on some level. I just can't say that out loud. It's scary. And I understand why she gets so scared, she has been dealing with this for as long as I have, and I know she is tired.

Step 5. Switch supervisee to the "self" chair. Have the supervisee reflect on what it's like to hear this and respond to the child client who is imagined in the "other" chair.

Supervisor:	What's that like for you to hear? What do you want to do for Julia? For her mom? Tell her.
Supervisee:	Julia—I am so sorry. I know that you need your mom. I will help her to be able to help you better.

Step 6. Switch supervisee to the "other" chair where she responds as the child client.

Supervisor:	How does the child respond?
Supervisee as client:	It feels good. (Let's out a sigh) Nervous but good. I feel grateful. I really want things to be better and I need your help. Please believe in us. I need you to believe in us.
Supervisor:	Do you have a sense as to what is needed at this point in time?
Supervisee:	[laughing] I've got to call that mom . . . Show her the compassion she deserves. Show her the compassion that she needs so that she can get unstuck too.
Supervisor:	And how do you feel about that?
Supervisee:	To be honest, a bit embarrassed. And really nervous (laughter). But I know it's the right thing to do.

Integrating EFT and EFFT

For EFT-trained clinicians learning EFFT, there is an option to use both approaches together with impressive fluidity. Should the clinician feel that a deeper processing of the block is necessary, more traditional EFT chair work can be integrated into the therapy. This approach honours the tradition in EFT of a *lifetime learning model*, whereby clinicians who so desire can enhance their skill set and seek to deepen their facility to utilize emotion-focused techniques.

The following is a clinical vignette illustrating EFT chair work in the context of EFFT to support a mother whose resentment (resulting from her own childhood wounds) made her unable to attend to her daughter. The clinician offered support and very brief EFT chair work within one clinical session. The purpose of the EFT chair work was to identify, validate, and process the grief of losing her mother at a young age. In the process of expressing this, the client became aware of her anger in regard to being left without a caregiver. Processing and resolving this block freed the client from maladaptive resentment, and allowed her to be present for her struggling teen daughter.

The clinician begins with the mother in the "self" chair.

Mother:	I can't help my daughter.
Clinician:	Picture your daughter there (in the "other" chair) and tell her: 'I can't help you.'
Mother:	(begins crying softly) I can't risk getting in there and getting close with the possibility of losing you. Because you are the age I was when my mother died.
Clinician:	It sounds like you miss your mother a lot.
Mother:	I do.
Clinician:	Can we do some work on that? Can you picture your mother there and tell her how much you miss her? (Note the fluid transition from picturing her child in the other chair to picturing her mother.)

Mother:	I've worked on this a lot in therapies. They're always telling me to get angry with her.
Clinician:	You don't sound angry with her. You sound like you miss her. Can you tell her: 'I miss you so much'? (The clinician is aware that there is likely underlying anger as is common in grief. The key in EFT is to follow the presenting emotion, then proceed to process it or have it transform to a more primary emotion.)
Mother:	(crying) I miss you so much. I miss having you in my life. I missed you being there when I got married and when I had my daughter.

Switch client to the "other" chair.

Clinician:	Come over here (to the "other" chair). What does she (your mother) say when she hears this?
Mother in chair as her mother:	I'm so sorry I wasn't there. I see what a wonderful mother you are and what a wonderful girl my granddaughter is. You have done so well. I love you very much. And I'm sorry that I didn't leave you better looked after—that there was no one there to care for you.

Switch client to the "self" chair.

Clinician:	What happens when she says all of that?
Mother:	It feels nice. And (with a wry smile) I feel a little bit angry!
Clinician:	Can you tell her that?
Mother:	Yeah—I am angry with you. You left and I had no one. I had to manage completely on my own. It was awful. And it's affected my parenting of my own daughter.

Switch client to the "other" chair.

Clinician:	What does she say to this?
Mother as her own mother:	I am truly sorry. That wasn't okay. You should not have had to go through that.

Switch client to the "self" chair.

Clinician:	Can you picture your daughter there again? What do you want to say to her?

Mother:	I'm sorry I haven't been there for you. That's going to change.
Clinician:	It sounds like you're saying to her: 'I won't let losing my mother affect our relationship anymore.'
Mother:	Yeah—that is how I feel.
Clinician:	Can you tell her: 'I won't let that stop me from being there for you.'
Mother:	Yeah—I won't let that stop me from being there for you.

Switch client to the "other" chair.

Clinician:	How does that feel for her to hear?
Mother as her daughter:	It feels good. It's safer to open up.

Summary

There has been a call in the treatment of mental illnesses to include families as "critical partners in care" and to address "sources of intra-familial strain and the need for other forms of therapeutic dialogue to reduce it" (Strober & Johnson, 2012; Johnson, 2012; Johnson & Wittenborn, 2012; Johnson, Maddeaux, & Blouin, 1998). We propose a treatment that privileges the role of carers as active, primary agents in their loved one's recovery. EFFT is an emotion-processing skills-based approach that focuses on the development of self-efficacy in the experiencing and processing of previously avoided emotions, a deficit common among these individuals and their families. A simple two-day workshop offering parents a set of tools in the four domains of Recovery Coaching, Emotion Coaching, Relationship Repair, and Processing Emotional Blocks has proven effective in reducing carer fear and self-blame and increasing self-efficacy, known to be highly predictive of a loved one's outcome. The rapid growth and adoption of EFFT is testimony to the need to fill in the "missing pieces" in ED treatment. This new approach attempts to fill this gap by affording carers a significant role in their loved one's recovery and by facilitating the development of emotional self-efficacy in carers and their loved ones. Developed first as an adjunct treatment for EDs, the application of EFFT has expanded to general mental health, parent coaching, and clinician training. The research findings show promising results for individuals and their carers. As well, feedback from the clinical community has been overwhelmingly positive. Perhaps as a result of its origin in the "untreatable" EDs, clinicians training in EFFT have found it to be a source of hope for families with whom traditional psychotherapeutic approaches alone had not proven helpful.

Notes

1 Note that "support" may be validation/empathy or it may be limit setting. Parents sometimes overlook the lack of limits as something to apologize for to the child. It can be very empowering for a parent to acknowledge that they have not set appropriate limits for that child and will be doing so from now on.
2 See Chapter 7 for specific resources.
3 It is important to note that although carers can benefit greatly from a course of individual therapy themselves, this is not the point of the intervention, nor is it necessary or prescribed by the model, even when it may appear indicated. Rather, the work is specifically related to and singularly focused on the resolution of the block so that carers can support their child in the different domains of recovery.

References

Bodell, L. P., & Keel, P. K. (2010). Current treatment for anorexia nervosa: Efficacy, safety, and adherence. *Psychology Research and Behavior Management, 3*, 91–108. http://doi.org/10.2147/PRBM.S13814

Bulik, C. M., Berkman, N. D., Brownley, K. A., Sedway, J. A., & Lohr, K. N. (2007). Anorexia nervosa treatment: A systematic review of randomized controlled trials. *International Journal of Eating Disorders, 40*, 310–320. doi:10.1002/eat.20367

Dimitropoulos, G., Freeman, V. E., Allemang, B., Couturier, J., McVey, G., Lock, J., & Le Grange, D. (2015). Family-based treatment with transition age youth with anorexia nervosa: A qualitative summary of application in clinical practice. *Journal of Eating Disorders, 3*(1), 1–13. doi:10.1186/s40337-015-0037-3

Dolhanty, J. (2017). *Emotion focused family therapy: From here to there*. Presented at the International Society for Emotion Focused Therapy, Toronto, Ontario, Canada.

Dolhanty, J., & Greenberg, L. S. (2009). Emotion-focused therapy in a case of anorexia nervosa. *Clinical Psychology & Psychotherapy, 16*(4), 336–382.

Goddard, E., Macdonald, P., Sepulveda, A. R., Naumann, U., Landau, S., Schmidt, U., & Treasure, J. (2011). Cognitive interpersonal maintenance model of eating disorders: Intervention for carers. *The British Journal of Psychiatry, 199*, 225–231. doi:10.1192/bjp.bp.110.088401

Gottman, J. (1997). *Raising an emotionally intelligent child*. New York, NY: Simon & Schuster Paperbacks.

Gottman, J. (1999). *The seven principles for making marriage work*. New York, NY: Crown Publishers.

Greenberg, L. S. (2002). Emotions in parenting. In *Emotion-Focused Therapy: Coaching clients to work through their feelings*. (pp. 279–299). Washington, DC: American Psychological Association.

Greenberg, L. S. (2004). Emotion-focused therapy. *Clinical Psychology & Psychotherapy, 11*(1), 3–16.

Greenberg, L. S. (2008). Emotion and cognition in psychotherapy: The transforming power of affect. *Canadian Psychology/Psychologie Canadienne, 49*(1), 49.

Greenberg, L. S. (2010). Emotion-Focused Therapy: A clinical synthesis. *Focus, 8*(1), 32–42. doi: http://dx.doi.org/10.1176/foc.8.1.foc32

Greenberg, L. S., & Pascual-Leone, A. (2006). Emotion in psychotherapy: A practice-friendly research review. *Journal of Clinical Psychology, 62*(5), 611–630.

Greenberg, L. S., Warwar, S. H., & Malcolm, W. M. (2008). Differential effects of Emotion-Focused Therapy and psychoeducation in facilitating forgiveness and letting go of emotional injuries. *Journal of Counselling Psychology, 55*(2), 185–196.

Johnson, S. M. (2012). *The practice of emotionally focused couple therapy* (1st ed.). Abingdon, Oxon: Taylor and Francis.
Johnson, S. M., Hunsley, J., Greenberg, L., & Schindler, D. (1999). Emotionally focused couples therapy: Status and challenges. *Clinical Psychology: Science and Practice, 6*(1), 67–79.
Johnson, S. M., Maddeaux, C., & Blouin, J. (1998). Emotionally focused family therapy for bulimia: Changing attachment patterns. *Psychotherapy: Theory, Research, Practice, Training, 35*(2), 238–247.
Johnson, S. M., & Wittenborn, A. (2012). New research findings on emotionally focused therapy: Introduction to special section. *Journal of Marital and Family Therapy, 38*, 18–22.
Kyriacou, O., Treasure, J., & Schmidt, U. (2008). Understanding how parents cope with living with someone with anorexia nervosa: Modelling the factors that are associated with carer distress. *International Journal of Eating Disorders, 41*, 233–242.
Lafrance Robinson, A., Dolhanty, J., & Greenberg, L. S. (2013). Emotion-Focused Family Therapy for eating disorders in children and adolescents. *Clinical Psychology & Psychotherapy*. doi:10.1002/cpp.1861
Lafrance Robinson, A., Dolhanty, J., Stillar, A., Henderson, K., & Mayman, S. (2014). Emotion-Focused Family Therapy for eating disorders across the lifespan: A pilot study of a two-day transdiagnostic intervention for parents. *Clinical Psychology & Psychotherapy*. doi:10.1002/cpp.1933
Lafrance Robinson, A., & Kosmerly, S. (2015). The influence of clinician emotion on decisions in child and adolescent eating disorder treatment: A survey of self and others. *Eating Disorders: The Journal of Treatment and Prevention, 23*(2), 163–176. doi:10.1080/10640266.2014.976107
Lock, J., & Gowers, S. (2005). Effective interventions for adolescents with anorexia nervosa. *Journal of Mental Health, 14*, 599–610. doi:10.1080/09638230500400324
Lock, J., & Le Grange, D. (2005). Family-based treatment of eating disorders. *International Journal of Eating Disorders, 37*(S1).
Lock, J., & Le Grange, D. (2013). *Treatment manual for anorexia nervosa: A family-based approach*. New York, NY: Guilford Press.
Miller, R. W., & Rollnick S. (1991). *Motivational interviewing: Preparing people to change addictive behavior*. New York, NY: The Guilford Press.
Neufeld, G., & Maté, G. (2004). *Hold on to your kids: Why parents matter*. Toronto: AA Knopf Canada.
Schmidt, U., & Treasure, J. (2006). Anorexia nervosa: Valued and visible. A cognitive interpersonal maintenance model and its implications for research and practice. *British Journal of Clinical Psychology, 45*, 343–366. doi:10.1348/014466505X53902
Stillar, A., Strahan, E., Nash, P., Files, N., Scarborough, J., Mayman, S., Henderson, K., . . . Lafrance Robinson, A. (2016). The influence of carer fear and self-blame when supporting a loved one with an eating disorder. *Eating Disorders: Journal of Treatment and Prevention*. doi:10.1080/10640266.2015.1133210
Strahan, E., Stillar, A., Files, N., Nash, P., Scarborough, J. J., Mayman, S., . . . Lafrance, A. (in press). Increasing self-efficacy with Emotion-Focused Family Therapy for eating disorders: A process model. *Person-Centered and Experiential Psychotherapies*.
Strober, M., & Johnson, C. (2012). The need for complex ideas in anorexia nervosa: Why biology, environment, and psyche all matter, why therapists make mistakes, and why clinical benchmarks are needed for managing weight correction. *International Journal of Eating Disorders, 45*(2), 155–178, 24p. doi:10.1002/eat.22005
Treasure, J., Crane, A., McKnight, R., Buchanan, E., & Wolfe, M. (2011). First do no harm: Iatrogenic maintaining factors in anorexia nervosa. *European Eating Disorders Review, 19*(4), 296–302.

Treasure, J., Schmidt, U., & Macdonald, P. (Eds.). (2009). *The clinician's guide to collaborative caring in eating disorders: The new Maudsley method*. London, UK: Routledge.

Treasure, J., Smith, G., & Crane, A. (2007). *Skills-based learning for caring for a loved one with an eating disorder*. London, UK: Routledge.

Waller, G. (2009). Evidence-based treatment and therapist drift. *Behaviour Research and Therapy, 47*(2), 119–127.

Waller, G., Stringer, H., & Meyer, C. (2012). What cognitive behavioral techniques do therapists report using when delivering cognitive behavioral therapy for the eating disorders? *Journal of Consulting and Clinical Psychology, 80*(1), 171–175.

Warren, C. S., Schafer, K. J., Crowley, M. E. J., & Olivardia, R. (2013). Demographic and work-related correlates of job burnout in professional eating disorder treatment providers. *Psychotherapy, 50*(4), 553–564. doi: org/10.1037/a0028783

4 Emotion Focused Family Therapy in Practice

Mirisse Foroughe and Laura Goldstein

Introduction

In practice, EFFT can be used as little or as much as a clinician chooses—or as a clinical setting allows for. When clinicians are first learning the approach, or are within very closed or pre-determined systems of treatment, EFFT may be used to inform case formulation and identify areas for intervention: a clinician may look beyond parent "resistance" and recognize feelings of low self-efficacy in a parent bringing their child for treatment and support that parent to build confidence in their own skills. As EFFT becomes more integrated into the treatment process, it may be used as a powerful adjunct to other approaches, for instance using parent EFFT sessions alongside a child's CBT process. This is especially helpful when we have communicated a clear treatment plan to a family and they cannot seem to make progress on the homework assigned to them. For example, a parent reporting that they could not find the time or a way to implement exposure tasks for their child with anxiety may benefit from targeted EFFT support to build their confidence and sense of competence in implementing treatment tasks. For some clinicians, or when it seems to fit best for a particular family's needs, EFFT can be used as the primary "umbrella" approach to treatment, as outlined in Chapter 2, with other interventions integrated as needed throughout the treatment process.

In this chapter, we outline the "how" of delivering EFFT to parents and caregivers from the first steps through to dealing with common roadblocks. This includes introducing the model, delivering EFFT individually, setting up a caregiver workshop, and how to share the core psycho-educational components while addressing caregivers' emotional needs so that they can attend to their child's needs. This approach is referred to as a system of "cascading attunement" because of the parallel process between therapist and caregiver, caregiver and child. Intervention strategies and practical tips are provided, and illustrated, so that clinicians can begin to integrate EFFT principles and techniques into their work with families.

Engaging Parents in the Process

As clinicians working in child and family mental health, referrals for our services are usually made for a specific child in the family. This is the child about whom parents are very concerned. The child doesn't listen, won't go to school, has intense tantrums that go on for hours, hits himself when he is upset, is addicted to video games, and so on. At first, parents often see only the individual-level factors involved: the child is too sensitive, too demanding, or uncooperative. Some parents believe that genetics are the problem, and that the family history of mental health issues means that this child is doomed to suffer too. Our first job is to help the parent understand the child's mental health difficulties as resulting from many factors that combine to increase risk, and that the child's current challenges can be best understood as a collision of a whole system of risk factors that created the perfect storm. Along with this, we immediately present to parents the notion that they are their child's best hope for change (if the issues are behavioural/sub-clinical) or recovery (if a formal mental illness has been identified). In sharing this, we invite parents into the treatment process to the greatest degree that we can, beginning with just a few minutes at the end of a child's session (if we are already in the process of individual treatment or if parents/the system in which we work demand this) and then working to empower parents to take a greater role in the treatment process as we move forward.

Ideally, parents are asked to attend the initial session on their own, without the child. This allows for two things: 1) parents can speak openly about their difficulties with the child without the child hearing negative things about themselves or picking up on their parents' negative emotions about the situation; 2) we can speak to parental fear, anger, guilt, and shame that is so common when seeking help for their child; and 3) we can build a therapeutic alliance with parents and introduce the EFFT notion of attending therapy on behalf of their child. If we also want or need to see the child or family together, we can manage this in a future session. The first session can set the tone for all sessions to come and plant the seeds for parents being the primary agents of change. As well, we can share practical information about the logistics of the sessions: telling parents to expect that we will often see individuals, dyads, and everyone together within just one session, depending on what needs to be focused on moment by moment. This dynamic way of using the therapeutic hour is very different than traditional modalities, and it is helpful to explain this to parents right from the start so that they know what to expect. If parents expected not to be involved at all, or if one parent is unwilling at first, we may need to be patient and persistent. We can continue to reach out, explain how important their role is, and very confidently invite the parent into the therapy. Once parents are engaged and empowered, they are an unstoppable force in the service of their child's health and wellbeing. An EFFT clinician needs to be persistent and encouraging, believing that every parent wants to help their child if they believe they can.

What About Confidentiality?

Many clinicians and parents worry that involving parents means the child will not have a "safe" or private space. We propose that the notion that children need to be able to "have someone to talk to" instead of their parents is built upon the reality that, more often than not, the children needed to talk to someone *about* their parents, or because of not being able to talk to their parents about their feelings. Confidentiality is what we explicitly agree it will be in this particular therapeutic relationship. When we see couples or families, as clinicians we do not usually promise to keep secrets or allow one of the family members to have the privilege of confidentiality while the others do not, so why do we need to promise children that we will not tell their parents anything? Complete secrecy may seem like a great idea if the child or teen is afraid of their parent's reaction or is feeling very distant from their parent, but do we want to reinforce that fear and avoidance? If our goal is to strengthen the relationship between parent and child, we need to change the way that we explain confidentiality. First, we can tell each family member that we prefer to work in such a way that allows us to talk to each of them separately when we need to and all together when it's therapeutically indicated. We can ask children, in the beginning of treatment and again after they have disclosed something important or at the end of every session, if they are alright with us sharing everything with their parents, or if there is something they would *not yet* want to share. Their response will tell us what they are worried about sharing, and this is a marker for us to find out more about their emotions in regard to the parent knowing whatever it is. Consider the following information given to a teen in an initial meeting:

Therapist: In order to help your parents help you, I will work with them throughout this process too. I will sometimes meet with you alone, and with them alone, and a few times I may ask us to meet all together, but we will prepare for that and wait until you feel more comfortable. Even then, some kids prefer to have the conversations with their parents outside of therapy, or only to have a few minutes together in session. We can work all of that out. For now, I just want you to know that while I will not share the things you tell me with anybody else, your parents are the exception. Part of my job is to help them understand your needs better. If there's anything that you want to tell me that you would prefer I don't share with them, you can tell me and I will also remember to check in with you.

We have found that many children and teens easily agree to this arrangement. Even if the teen responds most negatively about sharing information, saying something like:

Client: I don't want my parents to know anything! I'm not agreeing to that and I won't come to therapy if you are going to tell them anything I say!

We can still respond respectfully while not tying our own hands in the process:

Therapist: Okay, I get it. The idea of your parents knowing things that you say or feel is pretty upsetting to you right now. A lot of kids feel that way too. Some people worry that their parents will annoy or nag them about what they said ... some know that their parents won't be able to handle it and may get upset. There can be a lot of other reasons that you may not want to share things. I want to understand your reasons more, because they are important. For now, I can promise you that I will not share what you say, but I will continue to work with your parents and what I learn about you will still help me to help them, while keeping your words private. Unless of course I am worried about your safety, and those other limits to confidentiality that we talked about.

When we start off therapy with a child this way, and proceed to work through their fears about sharing their thoughts or feelings with their parents, they often come to feel more comfortable with doing so, and realize that being able to show their true feelings to their primary attachment figure(s) is exactly what they needed. Of course, this process needs to be supported by the clinician, and Chapter 3 reviews the model that we can use in the EFFT approach to working with parent-child dyads or families.

Psychoeducation, Normalizing, and De-Blaming

Most clinicians would agree that a parent's emotional response to their child's mental health difficulties is an incredibly important indicator of prognosis, or at least how easily or not the treatment process will go. Prior research on parental attributions (Morrissey-Kane & Prinz, 1999) and more recent findings about the role of parental emotion in a child's treatment process (Stillar et al., 2016) suggest that *what a parent thinks and feels about their child's mental health can significantly impact the treatment process as well as outcomes for the child*. In general, the more confident the parent feels in their own ability to handle the child's needs, and the more positive they feel towards the child's prognosis, the better.

While this may seem simple, it is *not* very common for parents to *feel* confident and positive about their child's mental health difficulties when they initially present for treatment. And for parents having been through several treatment attempts with different agencies or providers, things can feel even less hopeful. In fact, parents and caregivers are likely to feel a strong sense of shame and blame about their child's mental health. There is still a great deal of stigma in general regarding mental health, and parents can feel doubly stigmatized because they feel responsible for their child's functioning and behaviour (Corrigan & Miller, 2004). On top of this, parents are dealing with the caregiver burden associated with their child's needs; whether for a father of a girl with anorexia nervosa having to miss work to meet his daughter at school for lunch, or a mother dropping off her child with severe separation anxiety at child care, a parent of a child with mental health difficulties endures high levels of caregiver stress.

For the reasons above, parents presenting with a child for treatment (or bringing their child forth for individual treatment) are often feeling anything but confident and positive. The EFFT intervention begins with de-blaming and de-shaming parents, often with the very first phone conversation or email correspondence. The core messaging needs to be: "You did not get your child into this, but you ARE going to be the one that gets them out."[1] This is to address the fact that the parent probably a) feels to blame for their child's difficulties and b) feels powerless to help their child. (Stillar et al., 2016). So the very next core message to parents is: "And we will believe in you until you believe in yourself!"

Alongside the process of de-blaming parents, EFFT serves to de-pathologize the child. While a formal clinical assessment and diagnosis can still be part of the process, especially in a clinical setting that is designed for individual treatment of children or needs for formal labels within the child's system, the communication of any diagnosis or feedback given to parents is an opportunity to address the parent's feelings of guilt and helplessness, and the fear that their child is not "normal" and beyond help. As EFFT clinicians, we raise these issues with parents directly and with empathic attunement, following their own communication of fears, doubts, concerns, resentment, helplessness, and so on. Often, these feelings first arise when we ask parents into the treatment process.

Empowering Parents

When they are asked to take a leadership role in their child's recovery, most parents tell us that this is something "best left to the professionals." This is an understandable reaction, as parents and caregivers strive to do what is in the best interest of their child. Shifting the primary responsibility in mental health recovery from the clinician to the parent is a rather terrifying suggestion at first. It can help tremendously for clinicians to use analogies, metaphors, anecdotes, and hard evidence to counter these fears. Boachie and Jasper (2011) provide an excellent compilation of these for parents supporting a child through an eating disorder. Clinicians working with caregivers to support children with other mental health difficulties can use similar methods and come up with direct and indirect means of sending the message that parents need repeatedly to hear: their child needs their help, even if they are pushing it away or if it seems that someone else would be better for the job. Some parents feel immediately empowered when a professional simply gives them permission to take ownership of the tasks of the child's recovery, but many need more encouragement and support to believe in their ability to heal their child.

Pro-Caregiver Research Findings

The history of literature on parents and their child's mental health is rich with examples of how primary caregivers can mess up a child: "refrigerator moms" causing schizophrenia (Bateson, Jackson, Haley, & Weakland, 1956), "toxic families" (Rushton & Kraft, 2013), dysfunctional families (Kintner, Boss, & Johnson, 1981), and "parentectomies" being needed so that children can be properly helped by professionals (Vandereycken, Kog, & Vanderlinden, 1989) are just a few examples of the anti-caregiver messaging that certainly continues to impact how parents and caregivers see themselves and their capacity to be of good to a child when experts must know better.

To begin to counter this legacy of anti-caregiver messaging, we can share research findings that highlight the positive impact of primary caregiver involvement in child health outcomes. In 2013, O'Brien et al. published a ground-breaking research study in which parents of infants admitted to the Neonatal Intensive Care Unit (NICU) were asked to take over their daily care in hospital. We can ask caregivers how they would feel as the parent taking over care, as an NICU nurse handing over care, and as the infant in NICU receiving the care in this context. The knee-jerk response for parents is to say that they would feel terrified and ill-equipped to care for their child, and that the nurses would certainly agree that parents are not equipped to care for these fragile infants. However, when taking the perspective of the infant, parents can imagine that all the baby wants and needs in this scary environment is the warmth and comfort of their parent.

And what this research study found—perhaps to the amazement of the parents and health professionals—is that infants having their primary caregiver as "nurse" were found to demonstrate more positive health outcomes in every category (decreased parental stress, increased infant weight, increased incidences of breastfeeding, and overall satisfaction with the program) as compared with infants cared for by highly trained NICU nurses.

This example is central to the core tenets of EFFT: children need their parents more than they need anyone else, and no individual is better equipped to take an active role in caring for their child than the parent. Even with what is arguably the most vulnerable population, infants in the NICU, empirical evidence demonstrates that parents, when armed with a little coaching, are *better* equipped to care for their child than any "expert" professional.

De-Blaming/De-Shaming Parents

De-blaming parents is central to EFFT, and of paramount importance if we are going to engage parents and caregivers in the process of a child's treatment. A few practitioners within the clinical community have begun to emphasize this, with taglines such as "It's not your fault. It is your job" when referring to a parent's role in a child's mental health difficulties (Post, 2009).

As EFFT clinicians, when we are presenting clinical feedback to parents towards the end of an assessment or consultation process, we can outline for parents the many factors that elevate risk and contribute to the manifestation of "symptoms" or mental health difficulties. These factors include: genetics, life stressors, emotion avoidance, "superfeeler" temperament, epigenetics, social and cultural factors, puberty, and the family environment. When parents are then asked to identify the factors that we can have a high degree of control over, they are quick to realize that the two factors under their control are emotion avoidance and family environment. And, we can tell them, this is why we call it "*Emotion* Focused *Family* Therapy." This illustrates for parents that while causal factors are complex and multi-faceted—and caregivers do not cause their child to get to this place of distress or dysfunction—they are the ones that the child can count on to get out.

Parents Want to Know: Why Focus on Emotion?

What a distressed or dysregulated child needs most is a calm, regulated adult. Of course, it is anything but easy to stay calm during the storm of a child's emotional dysregulation. It can help for parents to focus on the emotions of the child, as these are what are propelling whatever behaviour the parents are concerned about. Focusing on the external behaviour, without understanding the root emotional cause, can lead to escalation of negative behaviours, and hostility between parent and child. After all, it is much easier to support a child refusing to say hello to a group of people when we see them as "socially anxious" than when we see "defiance" or "disrespect." Whether a symptom of mental illness, such as over-restrictive eating, shutting down in depression, or sub-clinical difficulties such as explosive, angry outbursts, these are all considered to be *symptoms* that are indicative of an underlying emotional difficulty. As is often the case, parents will complain about a specific behavioural manifestation of the core maladaptive emotion: school refusal in a child with fear of socializing or binging and purging in a teen unable to tolerate feelings of anger and shame. What we want to help them do is examine the underlying driver of the symptom(s). What is it that drives the behaviour? What is the child experiencing that is making them act this way? What is at the core? While it is important to address behaviour/interrupt symptoms, it is just as important to identify the core negative emotions that resulted in symptoms being necessary in the first place. Much like an antibiotic, EFFT works on the root level. Consider when someone gets a throat infection: they may present with a number of different symptoms such as sore throat, fever, and aches. We could elect to treat the individual symptoms with a pain killer, but we would just be masking the problem. An antibiotic targets the underlying root of the problem—targets the infection itself. So too does EFFT go beneath the symptoms (or presenting concerns) to target the difficult core emotions with which the child needs to build proficiency to identify, express, and regulate.

Emotion Basics

This psychoeducational component allows the clinician the opportunity to provide information to the caregivers regarding emotions. Too often, emotions are dismissed as weaknesses clouding our judgement or behaviour—people say "he was being too emotional" or "her emotions got in the way." In fact, emotions always control our response to the world, whether they are intense emotions such as rage or terror, or milder ones such as satisfaction or curiosity. Emotion is also our primary communication system with other people; we feel other people's intentions through their automatic emotional expressions (tone of voice, gestures, and other nonverbal cues) even when their words are telling us something different.

Emotions provide us with important information about our environment. They will us to action (James, 1890). The meaning of the word *emotion*, as we have come to understand it, was first used in 1602 and indicates an "agitation of the mind or an excited mental state." However, in the mid- to late 1500s the word "emotion" was more akin to definitions involving unrest, disturbance, and, most importantly, *movement*. If you remove the "e" from emotion one can more easily understand its etymological roots (*Oxford English Dictionary* 2009). Emotions signify movement or shifting within a person's being and should be understood as a signal or motivation to bring about a change in circumstance. We want to share with parents that emotions trigger physiological changes, and that it is not possible to "just stop" an emotion—it needs to run its course or be transformed by another emotion. We have to change emotion with emotion—accept our child's current feeling and help them feel something else.

As outlined in Chapter 3, parents being coached in EFFT learn that every emotion has three components: a bodily felt sense, a need, and an action tendency. For example, sadness feels slow and heavy, it needs comfort, and its instinctive associated action is to reach out for a hug. Failure to meet these associated needs causes frustration within the self, and this is when we see symptoms begin to manifest. This energy that is created by these emotions needs an outlet. *If this energy is not properly experienced and processed, the outlet and coping strategy becomes the symptom.* Emotion avoidance (i.e., trying to not feel what you're feeling) requires an immense amount of energy and is one of the root causes of mental illness. The symptoms inherent in mental health difficulties are viewed as maladaptive coping strategies that arise when one attempts to deal with strong negative emotions by pushing them away, distracting from them, or otherwise guarding against them. Alternatively, EFFT aims to replace negative/avoidant coping strategies with more adaptive methods, such as seeking out primary caregivers for support. Understandably, the most important factor in increasing caregiver-seeking behaviour is the child feeling that they are likely to receive an attuned response that will assist them in regulating; the need for a corrective and attuned emotional experience is the reason for clinicians to place most of their attention on building capacity within caregivers.

Until an emotion has been acknowledged and its associated need has been met, the brain will continue to signal us, and the body will not return to baseline. As such, an important step to Emotion Coaching is meeting the associated need for the child. A major roadblock to completing this step is the fact that a strong emotion in a child does not always make sense. Within the Western world, we place high value on logic, reason, and thought. We pay less attention to emotion, and this can get in our way. Consider this example:

> Jessica woke up one Saturday morning and, while still in bed, she discovered her university had failed to file some paperwork on time to defer a course that she was taking, and she received an "F" in this course. She was devastated. Now, this situation would be easily remedied, and despite the fact that she knew this, she began to cry out of frustration and disappointment. Her partner walked into their bedroom and, after Jessica had explained the story, he responded with "Don't worry darling, we can totally fix that." While fundamentally reasonable, this fact did not make her feel better. She was sad, and what sadness needs is comfort. Logic has no place when emotions are so activated, so Jessica was not at all soothed by her partner's response. A moment later, their dog, Misty, walked into the room, jumped on the bed, lay down on top of Jessica, and began licking her face. Jessica immediately felt better. Sadness needs comfort, and that is exactly what she received from Misty. This dog did not care why Jessica was crying—only that she was crying. By focusing on the emotion and its need, instead of its correctness or reasonableness, we can help emotions be successfully processed.

This anecdote can be shared with parents and caregivers, not to send the message that "Emotion Coaching is so easy, even a dog can do it" but that Misty was so easily able to meet sadness's need because dogs are not burdened with logic, reason, and critical-thinking abilities. This story seems to free parents who find themselves frustrated when faced with a child's strong emotions that they cannot understand because the message becomes that *they do not need to understand why their child is experiencing a strong negative emotion.* We do not argue with emotions. Emotions are always valid. When logic, reason, and critical thinking are removed from the equation, the task of validating and meeting the associated need becomes clear and simple.

De-Pathologizing the Child

Many parents want to know "why this child?" or feel strongly that something is very wrong with their child. Some parents report that their child has been "defiant since birth." They may have other children and those children are not experiencing such difficulties. Or they may compare their child to other children at their school, or in the extended family. Either way, it's hard for them to understand how other children have experienced the same or "worse" stressors in their lives and not developed symptoms. This can convince parents that their child is lazy, unmotivated, resistant to help, their own biggest obstacle, or—at worst—a lost cause. If we are honest with ourselves, these are the very things that we as clinicians may sometimes feel about parents.

To acknowledge the high sensitivity and intense emotional reactions that parents are seeing in their child, the EFFT clinician ignores the pathologizing labels or moral condemnations that children receive and replaces these with the term "superfeeler." The superfeeler is a person, child or adult, wired to be more sensitive to the environment in which they exist.[2] They think, feel, and sometimes react more strongly to events as well as to strong emotions (both their own emotions, and the emotions of others), and are often very good at hiding the fact that they feel so strongly. They can sometimes be more sensitive to external stimuli (light, sound, touch), and are more sensitive to perceived threats from the environment. These individuals are more likely to find ways to reduce pain and avoid emotions. They require support from their environment until they develop the advanced skills to process intense emotions on their own. Superfeelers are also highly likely to succeed in the arts and in caring professions and may perform unusually well in the world once they learn how to manage the emotions that they sense in others and feel within themselves.

For some parents, the term superfeeler and its defining traits are immediately accepted, and a relief to learn about, because they so precisely describe the child they have been concerned about. For the parents of an angry, highly defended child, the child seems anything but sensitive and empathic. In this case, it is helpful to share with parents that some superfeelers use anger as an effective mask for more vulnerable emotions, such as sadness, fear, shame, self-doubt, guilt, and frustration. These superfeelers can hide in plain sight, pushing away with their irritable and angry disposition the very support they desperately need from their parents. We can ask parents to imagine the child at age 2, or to go underneath the anger in some other manner, so that they can begin to connect with what the child needs.

Teaching the Steps of EFFT in Context: Clinical Illustration

Rose is a mother of a 15-year-old boy, James, and he has recently been truant from school and is beginning to abuse substances and hanging out with a group of kids known for having trouble with the law. You meet the teen for an individual session in order to learn about him, and you hear that he hasn't seen his father for over a year, even though his dad lives in the same city. James tells you that his parents divorced when he was 7, at which time Rose experienced a nervous breakdown, lost her job, and moved herself and her son to Greece for four years because she needed to be back home to recuperate from the divorce. James missed his father so much that he remembers crying himself to sleep every night for the first year. He didn't dare tell his mother how he was feeling, because he could see that she was doing better and happy to be with her family. During this time, James attended a French-language school, and upon returning to Ontario he was behind in reading and writing. As well, the other children made fun of his accent, his clothes, and the fact that he didn't know about the TV shows, games, or activities that were part of popular culture in North America at the time. When James tried to tell his mother about his troubles at school, he was told that he needs to "be himself" and just try to get along with people. While Rose felt overwhelming guilt for hurting James by taking him away from his father and the life that he knew, she had not talked to James about this and instead endured his increasingly bad behaviour, including physical aggression and bringing illicit drugs into the home. She also gave in, again out of guilt, when James asked her to buy alcohol for him to share with his friends so that they would want to hang out with him. James also talks to you a lot about his father, and tells you that all he has ever wanted is to know that his parents love him, and instead his mother is scared of him or feels sorry for him, and his father hates him and has abandoned him. In your office, he breaks down in tears, and you can see that he feels so ashamed and alone. As a child and family clinician, you make the difficult step of reaching out to James' father, Phillipe, and invite him into the therapy process. Phillipe tells you that he feels completely shut out of James' life and that Rose has always had the control. When you ask if he has tried to have a role in his son's life, he tells you that he has, but that James refuses his phone calls, doesn't answer his texts, and is rude to him when they do see each other. Phillipe says that James, being 15 and not a little child anymore, cannot be forced and needs to make an effort to have a relationship with his father.

Knowing how lonely, scared, and abandoned James feels, you know that he is not going to be the one to make the first move. You want the parents to assume this responsibility, but they won't. As a clinician, you have a few options: if you are a highly assertive clinician, you might invite the parents into your office and strongly advise them to a) take control and set limits for their son and be more involved in his life or b) let their son face the natural consequences of his actions in relation to drugs/illegal behaviour so that he can "hit bottom" and have a good enough scare that he becomes willing to get help. The parents tell you that they know they are failing their son and they will try to change, but the pattern continues to repeat, and you all become frustrated and discouraged. You might tell the parents that you cannot help them because they aren't taking your advice, or the parents might quit therapy because "it's not working."

If you don't feel comfortable being this direct as a clinician, you might repeatedly meet with the parents and try to convince them to take a stronger role, give them advice, explain how James is probably feeling, and watch hopelessly as the pattern repeats again and again until the parents or yourself give up on the process. In the EFFT approach, we find another option to working through parent-child conflict in relation to a child's mental health symptoms and successfully engaging parents in the treatment process.

In Chapter 3, we discussed the four core tenets of EFFT: Emotion Coaching, Relationship Repair, Recovery Coaching/Symptom Interruption, and Processing Emotional Blocks. At this point, an EFFT clinician would introduce the first three concepts to the parents, and assist them in working through each step so that they feel confident and empowered to take the first step in changing negative reactionary patterns in their relationship with their son. The clinician will also spend some time teaching the parent(s) when to use each strategy in context:

- *Emotion Coaching*: When the child is experiencing an intense negative emotion.
- *Relationship Repair*: When the present emotional experience of the child is neutral, the parent will engage this conversation with the child.
- *Recovery Coaching/Symptom Interruption*: When the child is engaged in negative behaviour that the parent wishes to correct (parent wants the child to either engage in a positive behaviour or disengage from a negative behaviour).

In James' case, Relationship Repair is an excellent place to begin this work, as it acts as a powerful "reset" button, with parents sharing the burden with him and showing that they can handle his anger, sadness, and shame. The completely non-self-referential apology opens the door for the expression of neglected or disowned emotions, healing, and emotional transformation. The first step is for the parent to acknowledge the unique impact of the emotional injury. The clinician helps guide the parent to think about what event(s) in the past might have contributed to a pattern of emotional avoidance: what should the child have been angry, ashamed, scared, or sad about but could not tell you or show? What negative feelings did they try to show but you could not see? Parents are supported through the process of "feeling in the dark" until they are able to open the "vault" of emotion. The process of Relationship Repair begins with the parent presenting an apology as a gift to the child, without any expectations and without needing to ascribe even 1% of the "blame" to anyone else but the parent giving the apology. The steps of the apology are:

1) *Acknowledge the unique impact of the emotional injury*: "When we moved to Greece, you were suddenly cut off from everything you knew and in a new environment. That wasn't what you needed."

2) *Express appreciation for what it must have been like*: "We left everything behind: your friends, family, school, and even your father. You had nothing in your life that was familiar anymore and that must have made you feel angry, or scared, or alone."[3]
3) *Apologize and communicate remorse*: "I am so sorry that I took you away from the life you knew and didn't allow you to show how painful that was for you. I should have acknowledged your feelings about the move and helped you through them" OR "I should have found a way to manage our life together in Canada so you could be close to your dad and everything familiar to you."
4) *State what could have been done instead*: "From now on, I will come and talk to you if I need to make a decision about big life events that affect you."
5) *Validate the reaction*:[4] a) Blast of anger: "Yeah, it was your fault and you ruined my life! I will never forgive you!"; b) Denial of parental blame: "No, Dad, it's not your fault. Mom took me away and you didn't do anything wrong." or c) Silence.

- Whatever the reaction is, validate it and repeat steps 2–4.

These steps can be flexibly applied for different circumstances. His mother could have apologized for not working out a workable visitation schedule with James' father, or for not setting stricter limits surrounding James' use of drugs and alcohol, or for dismissing his struggle by telling him to just "be himself" when he was having difficulties adjusting in a new school. This exercise helps families to rebuild trust and reset patterns of misattunement, and allows for less resistance when engaging in Emotion Coaching and Symptom Interruption.

Although each task is outlined with just a few simple steps, the process is rarely easy. When parents engage in each task, difficulties or "blocks" are likely to arise depending on if the parent is more fear based or shame based. These blocks provide the clinician with important information about the parent, attachment style, and historical context of the family and should be used as a signal to the clinician that deeper processing work is in order.

Engaging Emotion in the Process

The processing of live emotions in session is a core practice within emotion-focused approaches. The use of chair work in EFFT has developed from similar methods used in EFT and, earlier, Gestalt therapies (Wagner-Moore, 2004). The empty chair is used to engage the client in entering an imagined experience, which may be intrapersonal (within the self) or interpersonal (between the self and another person). This type of exercise can evoke the emotions brought up by experience, making them accessible for therapeutic intervention (see Chapters 1, 3, and 7 for detailed illustrations). Chair work allows clients to separate themselves from what may be holding them back from engaging in the process, in addition to allowing them to speak from the perspective of their child, partner, blocker, or other significant individual.

Integrating EFFT Into Practice

For a clinician working directly with emotion and harnessing the power of the family, the EFFT model provides fluidity and flexibility, and it can be applied to almost any treatment approach (CBT, DBT, behavioural, etc.) It can be used with parents alone, with child-parent dyads or triads, or with the family together. EFFT is also frequently used within a workshop setting in order to target high-needs/low-income families and is an excellent option for families with limited access to treatment.[5]

Consider, once again, the case of Rose and her son, James. The clinician would opt to begin treatment individually with parents if James was unwilling to attend treatment himself or if the clinician feels like beginning with parents would prevent a further sense of self-blame for James. Beginning with parents alone provides the added benefit of allowing James to feel de-stigmatized because his parents are learning to take radical responsibility. If James is willing to attend treatment, another option is to engage in parent-child dyadic or triadic sessions. This will allow the clinician to see James separately in order to collect information and understand his perspective and needs, while seeing the parents in parallel to build their capacity to support their son's emotional needs. If the family is willing and able to attend sessions together, the clinician may decide to offer a few family sessions in order for James to have a different (corrective) emotional experience with his parents. These sessions would allow James to share his feelings with his family and have those feelings be accepted, acknowledged, validated, and fully owned by his parents. If time and finances dictate that individual, parent, child, or dyadic/triadic sessions are prohibitive, having parents attend an EFFT caregiver workshop is an excellent option.

Caregiver Workshop Delivery

Delivering EFFT within a workshop setting has several benefits for clinicians and workshop participants. It allows the clinician to assist a larger number of families in a shorter amount of time. For the participants, this method is a time-efficient and cost-effective method of receiving intensive support that can immediately be applied to the difficulties they are experiencing with their child. The workshop setting also provides powerful social support from other caregivers, and this lessens stigma and feelings of being the "only one going through this." A recent study of 129 caregivers found that over 95% of participants were extremely satisfied with the EFFT workshop, and many caregivers described their experience of the two-day workshop as "life changing," "exactly what we needed," and that they "have hope for the first time in years" (Foroughe et al., submitted).

EFFT workshops are, by design, intensive, and they can bring up emotions that are uncomfortable, unexpected, and in need of adaptive processing. Trauma-informed therapy necessarily includes additional attention to details such as the physical environment, interpersonal interactions, and how to support emotion regulation in the process of delivering treatment. As the workshops are usually delivered to a group of 15–25 caregivers, some of the individuals will be highly emotionally expressive and ready to work through difficult feelings, while others will find the experiential tasks highly challenging. For one or two of the caregivers, the challenge can be too much to bear directly, and they will opt not to take part in any chair work or skills practice. As a facilitator, it is important to meet each caregiver where they are and gently encourage them to push slightly beyond that point. Even a 1% change in the parent will translate into a new trajectory for the parent–child relationship and the parent's response to the child's needs during this difficult time in their lives.

The physical space of the workshop needs to be large enough for individual seating and a surface on which to write notes (clipboards and paper are fine if tables are not possible for everyone), but not so large that caregivers can easily "check out" or avoid the emotional intensity of the intervention. We have found that close proximity to the facilitators and to one another helps foster intimacy, intensity, and togetherness, resulting in higher levels of engagement and processing during the workshop.

When delivering a workshop to such a large group of caregivers, each with high levels of caregiver burden at the time of the workshop, self-care and focused attention is critically important for the facilitators. Having two co-facilitators allows for a back-and-forth flow and reinforcement throughout the workshop. It is also helpful to enlist volunteers to assist in setting up the room as a welcoming environment, providing refreshments, preparing audio-visual equipment, and cleaning up after the workshop so that facilitators can connect with caregivers and answer their individual questions. When carers are participating in such an intensive intervention, having drinks and snacks on hand throughout the process is not just a luxury—refreshments and additional hands on deck provide support, structure, and relief from the difficult tasks at hand. Finally, the entire team—including assistants communicating with caregivers by email or telephone, registering and greeting caregivers as they arrive at the workshop, and any clinician-observers or helpers attending in order to learn—needs to be adequately trained so that they are cognizant of the potential sensitivities of participants. The clinical and assisting staff can be reminded to be warm and supportive towards participants, refrain from talking about anything to do with clinical process or their own learning while they are in the workshop room, and regulate their own reactions to things that they hear, protecting parents from feeling judged. It is not uncommon for parents to disclose personal trauma histories or incidents of abuse or neglect in their family of origin. Also, some parents find it helpful to share their most desperate thoughts, such as wanting to "throw the baby out the window" when referring to a colicky infant and four months of sleepless nights. As long as these expressions are symbolic, representing caregiver distress and not any immediate safety concern, the facilitator's sole focus can be on validating the caregiver's experience, normalizing their feelings, and ensuring that they do not feel judged by the clinical team. It can help tremendously for the clinician also to share anecdotes from their own life, including some reference to challenges within their own upbringing or from their experiences as a parent, aunt, etc. Caregivers always share with us that these disclosures helped them to realize they were not the only ones with an imperfect family life, and that we could understand and support them without any judgement.

Working With the Most Vulnerable Parents

Despite our best efforts at attending to the details of workshop delivery, difficulties will arise, and often they will involve some of the most vulnerable caregivers in the room. They may feel overwhelmed by the emotional intensity or attachment-based memories that other participants are sharing, finding that some of the content is bringing up painful memories that they had not planned to revisit. When feeling triggered, parents with a dismissing attachment style may seem sceptical or dismissive towards the intervention. Others may be openly hostile or may leave the room without saying a word. Often, feelings of self-blame or the fear of feeling other painful emotions underlie the caregiver's apparent resistance or distancing from the intervention process. Given this underlying vulnerability, it is critical that we, as facilitators, take complete responsibility for supporting these individuals in every way possible. This might mean approaching a quiet parent during a break, reaching out to a caregiver by phone if they seemed to leave upset or left early after Day 1, or in some other way connecting with anyone for whom we can detect the process is extremely difficult or painful. If we can validate their fears and provide them with support, we can make it possible for them to stay and work through difficult feelings. Many caregivers let us know afterwards that the facilitator's small gestures meant a great deal to them.

It is important to keep in mind that while some parents will make enormous headway, others can make a start or one small change that will begin a road of healing for their family.

Notes

1. In the parent workshop modality, parents are shown slides and presented with a model of how mental health issues develop.
2. This "wiring" can be due to genetics, intra-uterine experiences, early childhood stressors, etc.

3 The use of the word "or" here is purposeful to avoid the reaction of "don't tell me how I feel! You are totally clueless!" It sends the message that the parent is trying to meet the child where they're at, but without judgement or assumptions.
4 Typical child reactions to Relationship Repair are the blast: "It was your fault!", the silence: ". . .", the denial: "No, daddy, it's okay . . . you did your best!"
5 Further information regarding EFFT workshops is presented in the next chapter.

References

Bateson, G., Jackson, D. D., Haley, J., & Weakland, J. (1956). Toward a theory of schizophrenia. *System Research and Behavioral Science, 1*(4), 251–264. doi:10.1002/bs.3830010402

Bharadwaj, P., Pai, M. M., & Suziedelyte, A. (2017). Mental health stigma. Economics Letters, 159, 57. Boachie, A., & Jasper, K. (2011). *A parent's guide to defeating eating disorders: Spotting the stealth bomber and other symbolic approaches.* London, UK: Jessica Kingsley.

Corrigan, P. W., & Miller, F. E. (2004). Shame, blame, and contamination: A review of the impact of mental illness stigma on family members. *Journal of Mental Health, 13*(6), 537–548.

Foroughe, M., Stillar, A., Goldstein, L., Dolhanty, J., and Lafrance, A. Brief Emotion-Focused Family Therapy for parents. Submitted to the *Journal of Marital and Family Therapy*, October, 2017.

James, W. (1890). *The principles of psychology* (Vol. 2). New York, NY: Henry Holt and Company.

Kintner, M., Boss, P. G., & Johnson, N. (1981). The relationship between dysfunctional family environments and family member food intake. *Journal of Marriage and the Family, 43*(3), 633–641. doi:10.2307/351764

Morrissey-Kane, E., & Prinz, R. J. (1999). Engagement in child and adolescent treatment: The role of parental cognitions and attributions. *Clinical Child and Family Psychology Review, 2*(3), 183–198. doi:10.1023/A:1021807106455

O'Brien, K., Bracht, M., Macdonell, K., McBride, T., Robson, K., O'Leary, L., . . . Lee, S. K. (2013). A pilot cohort analytic study of family integrated care in a Canadian neonatal intensive care unit. *BMC Pregnancy and Childbirth, 13*(1), S12.

Oxford English dictionary. (2009). Oxford: Oxford University Press.

Post, B. B. (2009). *The great behavior breakdown.* Palmyra, VA: Post Institute.

Rushton, F. E., & Kraft, C. (2013). Family support in the family-centered medical home: An opportunity for preventing toxic stress and its impact in young children: Child health care providers offer valuable support and connections for families. *Child Abuse & Neglect, 37*, 41–50. doi:10.1016/j.chiabu.2013.10.029

Stillar, A., Strahan, E., Nash, P., Files, N., Scarborough, J., Mayman, S., . . . Marchand, P. (2016). The influence of carer fear and self-blame when supporting a loved one with an eating disorder. *Eating Disorders, 24*(2), 173–185.

Vandereycken, W., Kog, E., & Vanderlinden, J. (Eds.). (1989). *The family approach to eating disorders.* New York, NY: PMA Publishing.

Wagner-Moore, L. (2004). Gestalt therapy: Past, present, theory, and research. *Psychotherapy: Theory, Research, Practice, Training, 41*(2), 180–189. doi:10.1037/0033-3204.41.2.180

5 Processing Parent Blocks

Mirisse Foroughe and Laura Goldstein

Introduction

The concepts of caregiver and clinician blocks have been defined in previous chapters, along with an introduction to the methods for "processing" or working through them. The term *processing* refers to the EFT stages of emotional change, namely being able to identify, express, regulate, reflect on, and transform emotion in the therapeutic setting and in one's lived experience. Processing parent blocks is a psychotherapeutic technique that can raise anxiety for the clinician. In this chapter, we deepen the concepts and techniques that are involved in block work, provide case examples, and share practical tips for clinicians. While we focus here on parent blocks, it is as important for clinicians to have supervision and peer support in working through clinician blocks (see Chapter 2), and many of the themes in this chapter are applicable to people in general, whether in their role as client or therapist.

What Blocks Signify

With EFFT's central focus on supporting caregivers to free their child from the grip of mental health difficulties, the clinician will undoubtedly encounter parent fears and blocks as well as their own clinician blocks. Because the word "block" or "blocker" has a negative connotation, it is important to emphasize here that "blocks" always originate out of necessity; at one point in the person's life, these "blocks" were adaptive. Viewed through an attachment-based and trauma-informed lens, blocks refer to protective coping strategies that may have developed based on internal working models developed in early childhood (Main, Kaplan, & Cassidy, 1985; Bowlby, 1980, 1988; see Chapter 6 for a detailed account).

To honour and signify the survival-based origin of a block, the EFFT therapist can refer to this part as "the protector," "the guardian angel," or "the part that carries your pain," and talk about blocks in an accepting, validating way. Consider the "block" to be an entirely essential warning, like a traffic signal, telling a person to stop when something is unsafe. They had to learn quickly to obey the signal, or find themselves in a situation that could be harmful. At one point in a client's life, obeying this signal was adaptive. Today, it is getting in their way—often very quickly and without the person knowing it. It is the first job of the clinician to help bring emotional blocks into awareness, so that the caregiver is not trapped by an out-of-date, automatic survival-based process. To facilitate this transformation, one must interfere in the intergenerational transmission of attachment patterns. (See Figure 5.1.)

Talking About Blocks

When we know that the parent's own trauma history includes violence, and the treatment protocol now calls for them to set limits for their 8-year-old with intense tantrums, they may respond with: "I can't do it. He's too violent. He gets so angry and abusive—I just freeze." This is conceptualized as a "block" because it stops the parent from responding adaptively to their

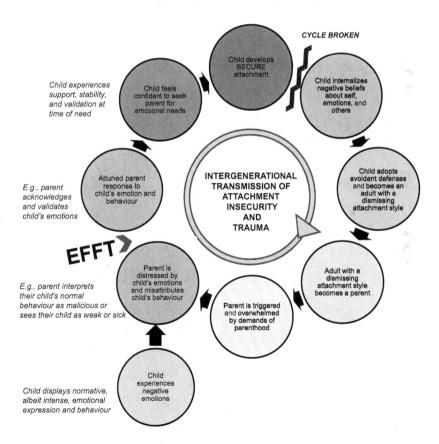

Figure 5.1 Transmission of Intergenerational Trauma and Attachment Insecurity: Breaking the Cycle

child's current need of assertive limits. We can then validate this block within an EFFT frame and say: "No wonder! Of course! The voice in your head tells you to freeze—that's the thing that saved you before." This approach is one of complete acceptance of the client's blocks, rather than trying to argue against something that developed for very good reasons. Validating the block not only reduces what we experience as resistance on the client's part, but also strengthens the client-therapist relationship because in accepting the block we are validating their lived experience.

Of course, we may not always know the parent's history. We can check in with them, we can use empathic conjecture, and we can attune to the messaging of their block to try and grasp what might be going on for them. We don't need to know the whole story—especially if this is a brief workshop delivery and there is not the opportunity to share complex history—but we can just ask, intuit, or guess that there was a traumatic event or subtle misattunement that occurred at some earlier point in their life. From a trauma-informed perspective, what matters is not the trauma itself but the *impact* on the individual.

Intergenerational Transmission: A Case Example

Katy was raised by her mother and father in a warm and secure environment. Her paternal grandfather, Walter, was a holocaust survivor; in fact, he was the only survivor from a family of 23. When the concentration camps were liberated in 1945, Walter travelled to New York to start a new life. Years later, he was married with two sons and had a successful career as a factory manager. Walter's long work hours in the factory also meant that he rarely had time to see his children, and, when he was home, he was a no-nonsense type of parent, attending to practical needs within his family but not showing much emotion or inviting closeness with his children. His lived experience taught him the value of hard work, as it was this value that had kept him alive. Walter passed on his work ethic to his children, and they were high achievers. When his son would come home from school with a 95% on his report card, Walter would not offer praise, but would simply ask, "*Where's the other 5%?*"

His response: "*Where's the other 5%?*" does not suggest a lack of pride in his son. On the contrary, this was a message of love and caring. He pushed his son to perform at his absolute best and to work as hard as he could because this value, to him, would ensure his son's survival in a world that, in Walter's experience, was uncertain and dangerous, with no room for error.

Moving forward a generation, Walter's son, Jeremy, took that lesson and instilled it in his own daughter. Katy grew up in a "tough love" type of household where the message that she received was, "*You have to work hard. If you want something, you have to earn it.*" This makes perfect sense, considering her family's history. The theme of needing to earn things permeated many aspects of Katy's everyday life. If she was standing in line at a grocery store and asked for a chocolate bar, she was told that she hadn't *earned* it. Once again, this was a message of caring in the perspective of her parents, as they wanted to instil in her the same principles and values in their daughter that was taught to them. However, this caring and well-meaning message morphed into a "block" in Katy's adult life, and she came to feel that she was lazy and unworthy unless she was constantly *earning* approval from important people in her life. While this message may have been adaptive in her family of origin, it became maladaptive in the context of Katy's personality, and she sometimes experienced bouts of depression, pulling herself out of a life in which she felt she was never good enough and did not deserve good things.

Examine the intergenerational pattern that emerges through this example. Three generations came to view hard work as a survival imperative, and in only one of these generations was this view an actual, physical reality. The subsequent two generations viewed hard work as a survival imperative insofar as it allowed them to gain approval, closeness, security, and safety from their primary caregivers. It is not necessarily the case that all "blocks" are born out of major traumatic events, such as child abuse, major losses, or the experience of other immediately terrifying events. It is more often the case that blocks are maladaptive generalizations of what was once adaptive in the person's earlier years. It is the mechanism that developed to keep them safe, secure, and connected to their caregivers in whatever way was possible. Taken out of this context, it becomes maladaptive and can "block" supportive efforts in the service of a child's regulation. *What a parent learned to do when they were a child is not necessarily what they now need to do to help their own child overcome mental health difficulties.* To illustrate this, when blocks have come into the parent's awareness, we light-heartedly ask them if they want to allow the 6-year-old part of them to parent their child today. Most parents see how illogical it is to put their inner child in charge of parenting or other "grown-up" tasks. However, talking about this is not enough—we need to help parents actually feel and transform the old emotions driving the block.

How to Recognize Parent Blocks

Blocks are essentially impediments or obstacles to the treatment process. When parents seek treatment for a child, they have an explicit goal for their child's health to improve. In the initial sessions, parents will often respond to motivational interviewing-type questions by telling us that they are "willing to do anything" to help their child improve or recover. The work of treatment, then, is whatever we need to do to interrupt symptoms, support the child emotionally, and generally meet the needs of a child. Parenting need not be perfect, and sometimes the changes needed are not big changes at all, but *anytime a parent's emotional response or behaviour does not serve the treatment goals, it is framed as a block.* Initially, a common block for parents with a trauma history is, "Don't get involved in the treatment," and the reason for that block could be anything from fear of pain or fear of shame: "It will be too painful for you," "You won't be able to handle it and then will look weak," to resentment: "You shouldn't have to get involved, this kid needs to take responsibility for himself. Nobody helped you this way when you were a kid," or fear of rejection: "If you get involved, he will hate you." The underlying emotions driving the block are powerful, especially for parents with a history of intrafamilial trauma; they will also interfere with treatment.

How Parent Blocks Interfere With Treatment

The child with an eating disorder needs to be fed, and any fear or apprehension about feeding the child is a block; the teen with severe depression needs to be validated deeply and then gradually drawn out of their bedroom and engaged in the world again, and the parent's apprehension about taking on the role of symptom interrupter and emotion coach is a block; the child still struggling to adjust to life four years after his parents' divorce needs to be able to fully express his anger, sadness, and shame, and it is a block if parents cannot validate these emotions because it would mean they are to blame for his pain; the child with a history of feeling rejected or bullied at school may need parents to be willing to face his negative emotions, and it is a block if it is too painful for the parents to agree with him that his experience was terrible, so they are cheerleading instead.

Main Types of Parent Blocks

Parent blocks can be categorized into two main groups: *blocks to setting limits* and *blocks to showing empathy*. The parent can "communicate" their blocks to us in many ways. For instance, they may share their concern through directly expressed hesitation at trying something in chair work: "I can't say that" or, "That won't work," or through the story that they tell us about how things are going in the home: "Every time I try to talk to him, he just screams at me and then I freeze," or through their nonverbal behaviour: when asked to picture their child in the empty chair, the parent's body becomes tense and they lean back, seeming afraid or reluctant. However the block is conveyed, it is a marker for the clinician to intervene. What the block tells us is that the parent needs our help right there in that moment, with that feeling—which may not even be defined yet—so that they can get on with the work of helping their child. This is the process of *cascading attunement*, meaning that the clinician attunes themselves to the parent's emotions, helping the parent process them, and then the parent attunes to their child's emotions. This process is a core intervention within EFFT, reinforcing that parents are the best people to help their own children with emotional needs, and that parents just need to have their own emotion blocks processed.

Blocks to Setting Limits

When a parent struggles more with setting limits, they may be afraid of the child's emotional reaction to being told "No," or worried that interrupting the child's symptoms will lead to a confrontation. The idea of a confrontation, and a child's extreme emotional reactions, can be very frightening or make the parent feel overly guilty or overwhelmed. Very often, the emotion underlying blocks to limit setting is fear—fear of rejection, fear of loss, fear of guilt, or core fear. We can conceptualize parents struggling with limit setting as being more *fear based*.

Examples:[1]

- Don't talk to him about the past. If you do, he will explode and you won't be able to handle it.
- Don't set limits about his computer use because he will just end up hating you.
- Don't enforce the house rules too strictly because she's been having a tough time lately and you're just going to make it worse. She will be upset and you will feel guilty.

Blocks to Showing Empathy

Likewise, when a parent struggles more with showing empathy by validating their child's strong emotional reactions, they may believe that they are not skilled at Emotion Coaching, that this just isn't their domain, and that trying to empathize will make them vulnerable in the midst of their child's strong emotional tides. Some parents feel worried about how expressions of support or validation will make *them* look in the eyes of their child. The idea of the parent being perceived as weak or "too soft" can be concerning, because parents fear that this will "over-empower" the child and maybe the child will lash out, say hurtful things, and blame the parent. Many parents with this type of block find it very hard to tolerate the idea of being blameworthy and have a strong negative reaction when asked to engage in the tasks of Relationship Repair, which involve apologizing to their child.

Example:

- Don't validate anger, it will just show your son that it's okay to always be angry.
- Don't apologize, because if you do, your daughter will take advantage and blame you for everything.
- Don't try to support him emotionally. You will fail and look weak.

Difficulties in showing empathy are most common for parents struggling with feelings of shame, whereas difficulties in setting limits are more often association with feelings of fear. The Parenting Dimensions handout in Chapter 7 is a resource to help parents and clinicians differentiate between the two styles. Of course, all categories tend to be generalizations based on themes and patterns. Some parents have what appears to be a "mixture" of blocks, and the most important thing for us as clinicians is to attune ourselves to the parent's underlying fears, shame, anger, resentment, and sadness—these are the usual suspects blocking parents from repairing the parent-child relationship, providing necessary emotional support, setting limits, and interrupting symptoms of mental illness in their child.

Case Example: Processing a Parent Block

A mother, Sue, attends a parent-only session for her daughter Natasha. Natasha has been diagnosed with Borderline Personality Disorder and has been suicidal, estranged from friends, and experiencing weekly emotional breakdowns. Her mother feels like Natasha would receive the best care from a professional, so she has been resistant to implementing EFFT with her daughter:

Sue: Please just tell me what you're going to do to help my daughter. This has been going on long enough and nothing is working. There is nothing that I can do to help and she really needs a professional.

Therapist: Okay, I want to try something different with you today. I want you to please sit in this chair and be the part of yourself that tells you that there is nothing that you can do, and that she needs a professional instead.

Sue: Fine. (Moves into other chair, speaking as blocker to the self) There is nothing that I can do . . .

Therapist: Be that part and tell yourself: 'There is nothing that YOU can do.'

Sue: Okay . . . there is nothing that you can do to help Natasha.

Therapist: 'Don't try to help her because if you do . . .'

Sue: Don't try to help her because if you do . . . you're just going to fail. You didn't go to school for this and you don't know how to make her better. She's too far gone for you to make any kind of difference at this point. Just send her to a psychologist and let them deal with her. If you try to help you're just going to make things worse and people will think that you're a bad mother.

Therapist: Okay, now switch chairs. (Sue sits in self chair.) How did it feel to hear that? What happens for you?

Sue: (Speaking to therapist) I agree completely. We came to see you so that you could make her better.

Therapist: Okay, so now I want you to picture Natasha in the chair across from you and I want you to tell her that you agree. You're not the one to help her, because part of you, let's call it 'the blocker,' doesn't want to look like a bad mother.

Sue: What do you mean? I can't say that to her.

Therapist: I understand it's hard to say, and I need you to say it anyway. If you want, you can even say, 'The therapist is making me say this.'

Sue: (Speaking to imagined child in opposite chair) I agree with my blocker.

Therapist: Tell her what you're going to do. Say 'I'm going to keep sending you to this therapist because you're too far gone for me to help you. I'm afraid of feeling ashamed and I'm going to make you do it alone. I can't help you because I don't want to risk feeling like a failure.'

Sue: I can't say that to my daughter. Ever. No. Absolutely not.

What did the therapist do in this case? Was she being too tough on the mother? At first, it can feel uncomfortable or risky to engage parents in chair work to evoke the emotions underlying their response to the child or the treatment process. This example illustrates that the EFFT process makes explicit the message that *this mother was already giving her daughter through her behaviour*. By bringing this message to awareness, the parent is faced with the reality of what she has been conveying to her daughter through her actions, or lack of action. It may take a couple of processing sessions, and we have noticed that it can be particularly challenging for mothers with a tendency to feel core maladaptive shame. However, with the therapist's support, this mother can experientially feel the fear of shame, followed soon after with the feeling of compassion for her daughter. In this way, the emotional experience of the fear of shame will be transformed. In EFT, this is conceptualized as changing emotion with emotion, and can only be done when the first emotion is activated (Greenberg, Rice, & Elliot, 1993; Greenberg, 2012). The parent's compassion for the child is a stronger emotion and can replace the fear of shame when the two emotions are experienced in competition with one another. The hoped-for result is that the parent's previous resistance to being involved in treatment will soften, and they will become more able to engage in the task of helping their child recover. In the process, the clinician may need awareness and support for their own "clinician block" which may be activated by the parent's dismissiveness, demands for progress in the child's therapy, and tendency to blame others (including the clinician) when faced with challenging tasks.

Don't Apologize Task

While caregivers start off the process pledging that they will do "anything" to help their child, as EFFT clinicians, we are occasionally faced with a specific type of block that seems insurmountable, resistant to all processing . . . *something* that the client cannot do or will not let go of. This is the caregiver's exception to all that they are willing to do—this is where they draw the line, and effectively this is where they are saying "I will do anything . . . anything but that." These strong convictions are frequently centred around their own ex-partner or parent. The "Don't Apologize" exercise combines the processes of working through blocks with Relationship Repair. Parents are asked to take 100% responsibility for an estranged relationship, an unforgiven significant other, or any other pain that they have held onto, even if the other person acted badly. This apology is in the service of their child's health. For example, the EFFT process may lead to the parent realizing that their child has suffered from animosity between their parents. When a child knows that one parent blames or resents the other parent, their grandparent, or another family member, this knowledge can be unsettling and breed insecurity in relationships, family life, and a child's view of the world. A highly sensitive child struggling with mental illness can be particularly impacted by the family environment and the relationships between their loved ones. However obvious this might be, it is often not enough to simply tell an angry parent to forgive their ex-partner because it's the healthy thing to do. The Don't Apologize task is an experiential chair exercise to use when a parent cannot will themselves to forgive or let go. The task enacts a conversation between the self and the part of the self that is holding onto the pain.

When caregivers are asked to take "radical" responsibility, it *feels* a lot like we are asking them to engage in self-blame. But a true apology is about healing the other, not wallowing in self-blame. In giving the apology, the client needs to feel empowered and hold a renewed sense of agency. If their apology comes from a place of self-blame, or they are just giving the apology because they are being asked to do so, further processing is required so that the person can forgive themselves. It is much more authentic to apologize when you have forgiven yourself for your part; all forgiveness is self-forgiveness.

Case Illustration: Don't Apologize Task

In this example, a mother of a child with an eating disorder was asked to apologize to her ex-husband to start the process of healing their relationship. She immediately refused to apologize, provided numerous examples of her ex-partner's bad behaviour, and insisted that he is the one from whom we should be asking an apology.

Therapist: Let's try something. Come in this chair and be the part of yourself that is telling you not to apologize to Ron.
Nina: You don't owe him an apology. Look at everything he did.
Therapist: Right, so tell yourself, don't apologize.
Nina: Don't do it, don't say sorry to him.
Therapist: Because if you do …
Nina: It will be a lie!
Therapist: Right. Don't give him a true apology! Because if you truly apologize …

Nina:	You won't truly apologize because you don't forgive him.
Therapist:	Exactly! Don't apologize to him because that would mean you are forgiving him, and if you do that, what will happen?
Nina:	If you forgive him . . . you would be crazy! He hurt you so much.
Therapist:	Yes, you are hurting. Hold on tight to that hurt, and don't let go. If you do something crazy like apologize and forgive . . . what would that feel like? What would it mean? Tell yourself what you have to lose by doing that.
Nina:	You would have to lose your pride, your self-worth! It would mean you are taking the blame for it all.
Therapist:	Right. You will feel to blame.
Nina:	And you hate that feeling! (Tells therapist: I don't like to be wrong.)
Therapist:	Yes, so tell yourself what to do instead of forgiving.
Nina:	Hold your ground, keep your guard up (voice cracks). Give him those judgy looks that he hates (laughs) . . . just keep letting him know that he's the bad guy.
Therapist:	Now come in this chair and tell your daughter the plan. Tell her that you aren't forgiving her father, and are holding onto the pain, no matter how that feels to her.

The purpose of this exercise, in addition to empowering the parent and relieving them of a heavy emotional burden, is to free the child of knowing that their parent is in pain. In his book *Wherever I Wind Up: My Quest for Truth, Authenticity, and the Perfect Knuckle Ball*, MLB player R.A. Dickey (2013, p. 269) quotes his therapist Stephen James:

> If you aren't willing to face your demons—if you can't find the courage to take on your fear and hurt and anger—you might as well wrap them up with a bow and give them to your children. Because they will be carrying the same thing . . . unless you are willing to do the work.

Processing Blocks for Individual Parent Coaching

Individual parent coaching sessions are essentially individually delivered EFFT. These sessions can be provided alongside a child's treatment, as a standalone parent coaching intervention, or when a child is refusing to attend treatment. Psychoeducation and processing blocks are involved in individual parent coaching as well, in addition to practicing the steps of Emotion Coaching, Relationship Repair, and Recovery Coaching. In each session, the clinician can engage in body sculpting, having the parent practice empathy and validation or limit setting, and processing of any blocks that arise.

Body Sculpting

Because so much is conveyed through body language and other nonverbal cues, body sculpting is a critical part of parent coaching. The clinician can ask the parent to share a recent incident that did not go well between them and their child. For example, perhaps the parent feels incapable of setting effective limits surrounding screen time for their school-aged child with ADHD. As the parent shares how the scenario usually plays out at home, the clinician will take note of the parent's body language, positioning, tone of voice, and other paralinguistic and nonverbal behaviours that may be incongruent with the desired outcome. If a parent is needing to set effective limits for their child, but their body is turned sideways as if they are ready to escape the room, shoulders hunched forward, and the message conveyed to the child is, "*I'm scared that this will not go well, and I don't feel confident that I have what it takes to actually enforce these limits*," then the child will be unlikely to take the parent seriously. Drawing the parent's attention to their body cues, and providing corrective feedback based on the context, can improve their confidence and raise the likelihood that their child will believe the parent means what they are saying.

While engaging in this sculpting task, the clinician can also pay attention to any emerging parent blocks. Is it difficult for the parent to act assertively? Do they seem fearful? Or do they appear distant, and find it hard to show compassion? Should the parent need more support than the sculpting exercise provides, the clinician will already have potential themes for the parent block task, which can then be processed.

Processing Blocks in a Workshop Setting

For caregivers to be able to engage in processing blocks in a group workshop setting, there needs to be a lot of de-blaming and a safe, supportive environment created by the facilitators. De-blaming and de-stigmatization are consistent themes throughout EFFT workshop delivery. From the beginning of the workshop, facilitators name the fears that a caregiver often has when attending a workshop: fear that they will be judged by others; fear that they will look like the worst parent ever; or fear that nobody has a child as far gone as theirs. Before any experiential exercises begin, facilitators share personal anecdotes from their own lives in order to demonstrate that no caregiver is perfect, family means forgiveness, and engaging in the EFFT model is a learning process that is applicable for all of us, throughout the lifespan.

Engaging the participants in chair work within a workshop setting can also engage other caregivers in the room to take on the role of the "blocker." The blocker chair is placed slightly behind and to the side of the parent chair, and the child chair is placed directly in front and facing the parent chair. The parent, with the guidance of the facilitator, selects a task with which to begin—Emotion Coaching, Behaviour/Recovery Coaching, or Relationship Repair. A co-facilitator or another caregiver can sit in the child chair and be the child. As the enactment progresses, the facilitator can check in with the parent about how they are feeling as they speak, how their child would react to the scenario, and what the parent blocker should be saying. The therapist then provides guidance to both the parent and the blocker throughout the enactment.

The "child" should be coached to make the scenario as difficult as possible for the parent, not easily resolving the task to provide parents with good practice for real-life situations. Additionally, the therapist should guide the blocker to be extremely assertive in their role, as it can be a challenge for a more timid parent, or one trying to spare the caregiver any negative feelings. This exercise serves to process the caregiver's emotions and, to do this, the emotions must be activated and accessible to processing. The exercise also provides an opportunity for skills practice and a learning experience for the other participants in the room. It takes a lot of courage for the first parent to volunteer for chair work, and other parents are often appreciative and express gratitude to the volunteering parents after the exercise is over.

Case Example: Caregiver Workshop

In this example, the facilitator is speaking to the participant sitting in the "parent" chair, unless otherwise noted. TR is attending the workshop to help with his 5-year-old daughter, Jacqueline. Although the registration form indicated that the child has separation anxiety, TR describes her as hyperactive and aggressive, with a violent temper. TR had travelled back and forth from the United States to Canada, working odd jobs and spending only a few months at a time with his young family. He is staying home in Canada permanently now but has had trouble connecting with Jacqueline. She becomes anxious when her mother is not around, and very clingy when she is. TR often becomes very angry with Jacqueline's behaviour and has been very loud and severe in his punishments. In the sequence below, the facilitator had suggested that they start off with the apology exercise:

TR:	So, I know that's a lot harder for her because of the way I was raised, I'm a more aggressive type, right. My wife was saying, she thinks it's more so that I feel like she's punking me off and that's why I get so um ... (hand gestures indicating that he gets worked up)
Therapist:	Workèd up.
TR:	Yeah. So that's my biggest issue at the moment.
Therapist:	Okay, so you want to do the apology for ...
TR:	Being so angry at her?
Therapist:	Being so angry. Okay, okay. And she can be, sometimes, really clingy with Mom like, like literally on top of her not letting go ...

TR: Like, back up in the womb . . . that's where she wants to be. (laughs)

Therapist: The insecurity, right? Okay so later we will work on reassuring her, but first apologizing for the anger and so, so your blocker, I guess, would be that part that says 'Kids shouldn't act like this and if you were a kid, this wouldn't have happened,' like right back to that kind of hard line parenting, or . . . ?

TR: Yeah, exactly that!

Therapist: (To the audience) Right! Okay so who feels like they could be up to that task? That kind of old school parenting and . . .

[Parent volunteers from the workshop. This parent has actually worked with TR before in a previous experiential exercise, where the roles were reversed and TR was his blocker.]

Therapist: Sure, please!

Blocker: (Taps TR on the shoulder) I got you.

Therapist: Okay. Okay brilliant. So um . . . so. (Talking to helper in the 'child' chair) Five years old . . . so lots of moving around and lots of . . . (Talking to TR) . . . what else would we see?

TR: She's defiant and she's like . . . any . . . it's pretty much just like anything I say she wants to go against it.

Therapist: Right, so lots of going against what you say? But doing the apology . . . we'll see what you feel she would do because she really hasn't had this before.

TR: That's true . . . so I don't really know how she'd be . . .

Therapist: So this is new, this is new, and I want you to just take it slow and, and we really appreciate you coming up and doing this apology. And remember, it doesn't mean that you can't discipline her sometimes and it doesn't mean that it's going to solve all the other things. It just . . . you're just saying sorry for being angry at the little girl, right? So I want you to picture Jacqueline there . . .

TR: (sits back in his seat)

[Here, we can already see that TR becomes immediately emotionally activated when imagining his daughter in the seat in front of him. The therapist checks in with TR.]

Therapist: Wow—what happens inside of you when you picture her?

TR: (Laughs)

Therapist: You really sat back . . .

TR: I start, yeah, I start getting a little heat inside. Start warming up in my chest.

Therapist: Yeah, yeah, of course. So it starts up right away, so can you . . . [speaking to the blocker] can you jump in for us? Tell TR, 'Don't get too close . . . don't let your guard down . . . you need to protect yourself'

Processing Parent Blocks

Blocker:	Don't get too close, protect yourself. Don't let her disrespect you. You're the boss, you're the one that's in control. You got to set her straight, she can't run the show.
Therapist:	Yeah. Otherwise, what? If you don't get your guard up, what will happen?
Blocker:	Otherwise, chaos. Otherwise . . . she's going to run the roost, she's not gonna know who's on top of the heap. You'll be the underdog . . .
Therapist:	Yes, Yes. And that means you'll be weak . . . you'll be vulnerable.
TR:	(nodding his head)
Therapist:	You're agreeing with him?
	[Laughter throughout the room. The laughter of the group serves to normalize the situation.]
TR:	Yes, exactly what he's saying. It's like he's in my head! (Laughing)
Therapist:	So, okay, okay (speaking to the blocker) so you keep it going, keep jumping in and reminding him to protect himself. That's really how he feels. (To TR) Now you can start.
TR:	So what do I start with?
Therapist:	Number one, acknowledge the impact of the anger she's seen (Indicating to begin with step one of Relationship Repair).
TR:	Umm . . . So Jacqueline, I'm sorry for letting my anger get the best of me.
Blocker:	Why do you think you need to apologize? You're the parent, she needs to respect you.
Therapist:	(To Blocker) Tell him: 'Don't apologize to her or she won't respect you, and you'll lose your power.'
Blocker:	Don't apologize to your kid, or you'll give up your power.
TR:	I know I shouldn't be taking anger out on you. You have nothing to do with it . . .
	[long pause]
Therapist:	'It must have made you feel so . . .'
TR:	It must have made you feel really scared and intimidated and . . .
Blocker:	Don't do it, this is dangerous ground! She's got to respect you! She's got to respect you!
TR:	. . . with me yelling at you like that . . . I didn't mean to get that way.
Blocker:	She's got to understand that you're the parent. She's got to understand that you're the parent. You've got to show her!
	[Here, TR is trying to say the right words but his body is highly activated, pulling back from the child chair in front of him, and seeming afraid and frozen. The therapist checks in with TR.]
Therapist:	I just want to check in . . . what's happening for you?
TR:	Tense, I feel tense.
Therapist:	Can you turn and face your blocker?
	[TR turns chair to blocker.]

[Here, the therapist asks TR to face his blocker in order to directly process the emotions that have come up while hearing these words. Here, the therapist will facilitate the interaction between TR and his block, in order to free him to allow for the Relationship Repair steps to be delivered. Through this segment, we learn some of the history that contributed to the formation of his block.]

Therapist: (Speaking to the blocker) Okay, I want you to say it again.

Blocker: This is dangerous ground. You're giving up your power. You gotta show her who's boss. If she doesn't listen to you there will be hell to pay.

Therapist: (Speaking to the blocker) Yeah ... and that will mean that you're just ... pathetic and weak ...

Blocker: You can't apologize to a 5-year-old, that's weak. She's going to be out of control and you won't be able to control her.

Therapist: Okay. I just want you to respond to that. What does it make you feel like when you hear this?

TR: Uhh ... I feel like I'm struggling with myself. This is the struggle ... should I get angry and protect myself?

Therapist: Okay, and what's the other side of the struggle?

TR: Just knowing she's 5, you know? She's a girl ...

Therapist: Okay can you tell him? Tell your blocker [points to blocker].

TR: (Speaking to blocker) She's 5, she's a girl, nobody deserves to be treated in a bad manner.

Therapist: (guiding blocker to respond) That's how you were treated! (Speaking to TR) Like, I don't know your history ... but maybe?

TR: That doesn't mean it's okay for me to do it. And it's not something that I want to carry on for my children.

Therapist: (Nods) Tell him (points to blocker).

TR: (Speaking to blocker) It's not a trait that I want to carry on for the kids. Um ... I was beat a lot as a kid and I think that's part of my anger problem but that's not something that I want to do to them.

Therapist: What do you need from this part of you (points to blocker). What would you need just to get through these five minutes here?

TR: Go away! (Laughs) Just leave me alone! Stop talking to me! (Speaking to therapist) Wow, that does feel good, though!

Therapist: I don't know the history ... if it was mom or dad ... but it's kind of like this part of you is so afraid and has become like ... 'I'm never going to feel like that again. If anyone threatens me ... even my daughter ... I'm going to show them!' So this is like the little boy part of you, isn't it (points to blocker), right? So speak to him ... reassure him.

TR: (Speaking to blocker) I don't need you anymore. I can do this myself.

Therapist:	Right, and imagine that's you at age 5. He was there through the beatings, and he found a way to survive by having his guard up. Now we are telling him 'I don't need you anymore.' How's that going to go for him?
TR:	No go. He's not buying that! He's going to stick to his guns.
Therapist:	Right, because he learned this lesson the hard way. He had to protect you. It was really scary back then . . .
TR:	Oh, yeah. Damn right.
Therapist:	Right. And I don't know if it was mom or dad . . .
TR:	Neither of them, it was my uncle.
Therapist:	Okay, and it was terrifying, you were a little kid. Just like you said about Jacqueline—you don't want to yell at her and scare her, and you were very scared as a kid. Imagine if that was her it was happening to?
TR:	No! That makes me so angry—I would never want that for her.
Therapist:	Right, you want to protect her. But he (points to blocker) wasn't protected and he came up with a way to protect you. How do you feel towards him?
TR:	I feel sad. I feel sad for him. No kid should have to go through that.
Therapist:	Right, so you feel compassion for him . . . so can you validate how scared he was?
TR:	It was really scary for you. I know why you always get my back up. It was terrifying. You never knew what was coming . . . he would catch you off guard.
Therapist:	Right, so it's like you understand why he gets your guard up so quickly . . . and can you reassure this part of you that you're going to be able to handle things and that he doesn't need to jump in and protect you every time? Can you tell him 'I know you're scared, but I got this? I just need a few minutes to parent my daughter and then we can talk more about this or . . .' (TR nods and laughs.)
TR:	Yes, you can have all night of my attention, but I need to help my daughter feel safe right now. Give me five minutes.
Therapist:	Okay, so let's try again. Turn back around to your daughter now.
TR:	(Leaning in, with a softer voice) Hey Jacqueline . . . I want to tell you something. I appreciate that it's scary for you to have your dad screaming and yelling at you like that . . .
Child:	Yeah . . .
TR:	I'm so sorry for that. I wish I could go back in time . . . can you stop moving around in your chair, please?
Therapist:	So I know you want respect, and you know that kids also show with their body how they're feeling, just like you were doing. How does it feel when she's moving around all over the place?
TR:	Yeah, it's that same fear like she's not respecting me.
Therapist:	Okay, so what do you need?

TR:	No, I'm good, I want to focus on her . . . she needs me to let her feel scared because that's why she's moving around. Kids don't just sit and listen to this stuff . . . do they?
Therapist:	Agreed, usually kids don't just sit . . . not at age 5! (TR and audience laughing) And she's still going to hear you. So back to step 2, then, 'It must have made you feel so . . .'
TR:	It must have made you feel so scared. I didn't want to do that. I'm going to try my hardest to not let it happen again.
Therapist:	Do step 3 first. Give her the actual words 'I'm sorry.'
TR:	(Dismissively) I'm sorry for being the way I've been.
Therapist:	Say it again.
	[The therapist instructs repetition at this point because apologizing was very difficult for TR, and he rushed it the first time. The second time, he is more attuned and saying sorry with greater intention.]
TR:	I'm sorry for all the anger and letting my anger come out the way it does. I'm sorry that you had to feel scared of me. My anger was scary and I am sorry for that.
Therapist:	Say what you should have done and will do from now on in those moments . . . 'When you misbehaved . . . I should have . . .'
TR:	I should have went about it differently. Maybe comforted you when I knew you were upset instead of getting upset myself. I wish I would have come to this workshop sooner. I need to control my emotions better.
Therapist:	And from now on . . . ?
TR:	From now on I'm going to do everything in my power to make sure that I don't let that happen again.
Therapist:	(Guiding blocker) 'Don't comfort her. She's going to disrespect you and you will be vulnerable . . .'
Blocker:	It's not going to work. Don't make yourself weak. You are the parent, you are the boss. Look, she's not even listening to you now! She's squirming around and ignoring you!
TR:	(Responding to blocker) You're not bugging me again (smiling).
	[At this point, we can see that TR is not as activated by his blocker.]
Therapist:	Okay, so tell her how you will make sure things are from now on, like 'Things aren't going to be perfect but I will make sure that you feel . . .' What do you want her to feel instead of scared?
TR:	Safe.
Therapist:	Tell her.
TR:	I'm going to do everything in my power to make sure that this doesn't happen again. I'm going to have more control over my emotions. I want you to feel safe and comforted. It's my job to make you feel safe and comfortable.
Therapist:	So now, we don't know how she's going to respond because this is so new, and she's 5, so you might want to suggest that you both do something fun together. Now, how did that feel for you?

TR:	I'd probably take her down for milk and cookies! I feel ... I feel so much better. I got things off my chest.
Therapist:	Yes. There was so much on your chest at first when you were sitting all the way back. Now you are leaning in ... (to the child) and what did that feel like to hear from Dad?
Child:	It was so comforting. When you told me that it's your job to make me feel safe and comfortable, I just felt like everything was going to be okay now, and you were going to take care of me.
Therapist:	Amazing—and (to TR) you did all of that with the kid squirming around, not even looking at you! Amazing! How do you feel now?
TR:	I feel hopeful. Really hopeful. Like I don't need to have my guard up all the time, and I can be a father to my daughter. Thank you so much. I'm so glad that I came to this workshop today.

Through this case example, we see how emotionally activated TR became when faced with his daughter and his blocker. Much of the activation does not come through in the written transcript of the dialogue, but was evident in his body language, nonverbal cues, and the emotion in the room at the time of his chair work. Afterwards, he seemed so relieved and much more relaxed. He spoke with other parents at the break, and referred to the workshop as a life-changing experience.

Summary

Participating in chair work, especially for processing parent blocks, can be a powerful and transformative experience and has a rich history within person-centred and emotion-centred modalities (see Conoley, Conoley, McConnell, & Kimzey, 1983; Greenberg & Rice, 1981; Mackay, 1996; Maurer, 2012; Lafrance, McCague, & Whissell, 2014; Shahar et al., 2012; and Sutherland, Peräkylä, & Elliott, 2014 for a review). There is no way around it, the "chair work thing" (Robinson, McCague, & Whissell, 2014) can feel strange or awkward at first—for the client as well as the clinician! With practice, clinicians will begin to feel more comfortable, and competent, at working directly with emotions. Read and re-read the case examples, practice with the worksheets provided in Chapter 7, and partner with a colleague to work through the clinician blocks that will pop up; soon you will find that chair work is a powerful tool for processing emotions—yours and your client's!

Note

1 Take note of the general theme of these thoughts—they are based around what a parent fears.

References

Bowlby, J. (1980). *Attachment and loss: Vol. 3. Loss, sadness, and depression*. New York: Basic Books.

Bowlby, J. (1988). *A secure base*. New York: Basic Books.

Conoley, C. W., Conoley, J. C., McConnell, J. A., & Kimzey, C. E. (1983). The effect of the ABCs of rational emotive therapy and the empty-chair technique of Gestalt therapy on anger reduction. *Psychotherapy: Theory, Research & Practice, 20*(1), 112–117. doi:10.1037/h0088470

Dickey, R. A. (2013). *Wherever I Wind Up: My Quest for Truth, Authenticity, and the Perfect Knuckle Ball*. New York, NY: Penguin Group (USA).

Greenberg, L. S. (2012). Emotions, the great captains of our lives: Their role in the process of change in psychotherapy. *American Psychologist, 67*(8), 697–707. doi: 10.1037/a0029858

Greenberg, L. S., & Rice, L. N. (1981). The specific effects of a Gestalt intervention. *Psychotherapy: Theory, Research & Practice, 18*(1), 31–37. doi:10.1037/h0085958

Greenberg, L. S., Rice, L., & Elliott, P. (1993). *Facilitating emotional change: The moment by moment process*. New York, NY: Guilford Press.

Lafrance Robinson, A. (2014). *Examining the relationship between parental fears and accommodating and enabling behaviors in parents caring for a child with an eating disorder*. Unpublished manuscript.

Mackay, B. A. N. (1996). *The Gestalt two-chair technique: How it relates to theory* (Order No. AAMNN06010). Available from PsycINFO.

Main, M., Kaplan, N., & Cassidy, J. (1985). Security in infancy, childhood, and adulthood: A move to the level of representation. *Monographs of the Society for Research in Child Development, 50*, 66–106.

Maurer, R. (2012). The power of the empty chair. *The Journal for Quality and Participation, 35*(2), 10–11.

Robinson, A. L., McCague, E. A., & Whissell, C. (2014). "That chair work thing was great": A pilot study of group-based Emotion-Focused Therapy for anxiety and depression. *Person-Centered and Experiential Psychotherapies, 13*(4), 263–277. doi: 10.1080/14779757.2014.910131

Shahar, B., Carlin, E. R., Engle, D. E., Hegde, J., Szepsenwol, O., & Arkowitz, H. (2012). A pilot investigation of emotion-focused two-chair dialogue intervention for self-criticism. *Clinical Psychology & Psychotherapy, 19*(6), 496–507. doi:10.1002/cpp.762

Sutherland, O., Peräkylä, A., & Elliott, R. (2014). Conversation analysis of the two-chair self-soothing task in Emotion-Focused Therapy. *Psychotherapy Research, 24*(6), 738–751. doi:10.1080/10503307.2014.885146

6 EFFT and Trauma

Engaging the Parent With a Dismissing Attachment Style

Kristina Cordeiro, Sara Lynn Rependa, Robert T. Muller, and Mirisse Foroughe

Working in children's mental health, we often find ourselves working with parents. Whether it's a few minutes at the end of a child's session, a phone call from a concerned parent, or with a parent whom we have invited into the therapeutic process, working with parents can be a challenge, especially if our own training has focused on children and adolescents. In EFFT, parents are called upon to be central in the treatment of their child. While this can be challenging for all parents, those with a history of complex, intrafamilial trauma often have particular difficulty with learning to be emotion coaches, behaviour coaches, and taking on the tasks of Relationship Repair and of their child's recovery. These parents often present with a dismissing (also known as avoidant) attachment style, and this can greatly impact the therapeutic process for their child.

Individuals with a dismissing attachment style rely on avoidance, or what we call "deactivating strategies," to protect themselves from psychological pain and rejection. They work hard to *not feel*, to not remember painful attachment-related memories, thoughts, and emotions, and to avoid interdependence, emotional closeness, and vulnerability in their relationships. Because these individuals tend to view themselves as independent, strong, and self-sufficient (Bartholomew & Horowitz, 1991; Eagle, 2006; Muller, 2010), they can be defensive towards receiving help, even when they or their children experience significant mental health difficulties and are seeking help through therapy. Of course, they want their child to get better, but they are not prepared to handle that they may feel worse, and face painful memories, in the process. Often, parents with a trauma history believe that they cannot be the ones to help their child, because they have to protect themselves and/or their child from dangerous emotions that the therapeutic process might evoke. If their child could just have someone else to talk to, they wouldn't have to be the ones to try and support the child emotionally or behaviourally. They wouldn't have to face their own trauma history, the possibility of failure, or their inability to help their child.

With all of these very good reasons to avoid emotional pain (their own and their child's), it's not surprising that therapy can be challenging and emotionally exhausting for parents with a dismissing style (Chu, 1998; Davies & Frawley, 1994), as well as for the therapist (Dalenberg, 2000; Muller, 2010;

Pearlman & Saakvitne, 1995). With this population, building a strong therapeutic alliance can be quite difficult right from the outset (Pearlman & Courtois, 2005; Muller, 2009, 2010, in press). Relatedly, even if we manage to forge a connection, as clinicians we may struggle to *maintain* an alliance with these parents. Parents with a dismissing style can feel threatened by the closeness and empathy developed in the therapeutic alliance, and will sometimes resort to protective actions such as not showing up to sessions or other distancing manoeuvres. This serves to protect them from the danger of becoming vulnerable with the therapist, but it also slows down and interrupts the therapeutic process for their child.

Activate and Challenge

In this chapter, we outline specific intervention strategies that we have been working on for several years at the Trauma & Attachment Lab at York University in Toronto (Muller, 2009, 2010, in press). The focus has been on therapeutic process and trauma-informed practice, including: addressing avoidance among people with trauma histories, increasing client engagement throughout treatment, working with emotion, and viewing the therapeutic relationship as central in working with the individual.

We illustrate *how* to effectively engage individuals with a dismissing style in therapy and to work with avoidant defences and painful attachment-related memories and emotions, providing case examples drawn from clinical practice. Our research in the Trauma & Attachment Lab has focused on intrafamilial trauma and attachment, as well as treatment process and outcomes (e.g., Foroughe & Muller, 2012, 2014; Muller, 2009, 2010, in press; Muller & Rosenkranz, 2009). Our findings confirm the importance of the therapeutic relationship (e.g., Zorzella, Rependa, & Muller, 2017) and highlight the value of actively involving parents in the treatment of their children (e.g., Konanur, Muller, Cinamon, Thornback, & Zorzella, 2015). Our approach to therapy prioritizes the therapeutic relationship, activating the attachment system, and challenging defensive avoidance. This "activate and challenge" approach gradually exposes parents to their emotional triggers and with support from the therapist, facilitates therapeutic change and prepares parents for the work to be done in their child's recovery (Muller, 2010, in press; Foroughe & Muller, 2012, 2014).

Understanding the Parent With a Dismissive (Avoidant) Attachment Style

Becoming a parent is arguably one of the most rewarding yet physically and psychologically challenging experiences of an individual's life. For the parent with a history of relationships built on fear and abuse in their own childhood, the demands for closeness, intimacy, and vulnerability in the relationship with their own child can be highly distressing (Foroughe & Muller, 2012). Caring for a child can trigger early memories of intrafamilial trauma.

Parenthood, by its very nature, directly challenges the deactivating strategies that people may have relied on for years. For these parents, routine, day-to-day caregiving responsibilities can be quite difficult, and parenting during times of stress can be especially overwhelming. This is because it takes a great deal of psychological effort to maintain avoidant strategies, which begin to break down when the attachment system is highly activated or repeatedly stressed (Dozier & Kobak, 1992; Edelstein & Gillath, 2008; Muller, 2010).

Without a child to care for, a young professional having had a challenging day at work can come home and de-stress by being alone, watching their favourite television show, or having a glass of wine. With a child in the picture, this de-stressing "alone time" naturally disappears or dwindles to mere minutes after the child has gone to bed, because the needs of the child rightly take precedence. The deactivating strategies the individual once relied on have become impossible to maintain, and the parent can become overwhelmed. For a parent with a trauma history, the typical temper tantrum of an unruly 2-year-old can be experienced as violent and threatening. Furthermore, the parent cannot retreat and hide from this overwhelming expression of emotion (as they did as a child hiding from the violent outburst of a parent) because their own child needs tending to. The parent can be left feeling overwhelmed, dysregulated, and ineffective.

When faced with their child's emotional needs, parents with a dismissing attachment style may appear insensitive or unresponsive, often discouraging dependency and expressions of vulnerability (Foroughe & Muller, 2012, 2014; Muller, in press). It is not unusual for these parents to minimize or altogether dismiss their child's emotional experiences. Compared to parents with a secure attachment, parents with a dismissing style tend to be less warm and supportive, and more controlling and task-focused when playing or interacting with their children (e.g., Crowell & Feldman, 1988). In therapy, things can become even more challenging for parents because they are now being faced with the demands of their child's mental health difficulties, painful emotions, and needs that sometimes run counter to what is comfortable for them (e.g., an unruly toddler needing firm limits from a parent struggling to be authoritative; an adolescent child blaming his parents for their divorce; or a young adult angry at her parents for not noticing that she had developed an eating disorder years ago). In some cases, parents with a dismissing style may over-respond by pathologizing their child's normal behaviour and emotional expression—seeing their "superfeeler" child as intolerable, too sensitive, too needy, disobedient, inconsolable, uparentable . . . broken in some way. Other parents may feel overwhelmed and scared of their child, unable to adequately set limits or soothe the child when she is distressed.

Clinically, this fear can reveal itself in subtle ways: Jennifer was a young mother of a 4-month-old daughter, Daniella. She initially sought support for her daughter's difficulties with sleeping and eating. Concerned about her baby's growth and development, Jennifer reported feeling utterly exhausted and overwhelmed by caring for Daniella, who frequently fussed or refused to eat while nursing, slept for only 20 minutes at a time, and had failed to gain a sufficient amount of weight since birth. During the family's clinical assessment and early therapy sessions, Jennifer consistently held Daniella facing away from her with stiff arms, and she would often put her baby down on a play mat shortly after arriving for the session. Difficulties within the parent-child dyad were most obvious when Daniella would fuss or cry. Although Jennifer would quickly try to soothe Daniella by picking her up or attempting to nurse her, in that moment, Jennifer's facial expressions suggested that she was frightened; her body was visibly tense, her speech haunting and wavering, and her physical hold while nursing Daniella provided little support or security.

We can see how Jennifer's fear, a response to much earlier trauma, impacted how she interacted with her child. Knowing how sensitive infants are to their mother's emotion states, it is easy to imagine that Daniella could have found her mother's behaviour frightening (Main & Hesse, 1990). Indeed, Daniella consequently remained unsettled, despite her mother's efforts to soothe her, and this negatively reinforced how Jennifer experienced her child and herself as a mother.

Some children are more emotionally reactive, more temperamental or sensitive than others. These emotional sensitivities can trigger the fear of dangerous emotional expression in the parent with a dismissing style. Over time, slight misattunement between the child's needs and the parent's response style can lead to the development of an insecure attachment (see Hesse & Main, 2006, for a review). Examples of misattunement include unresponsiveness when a child is needing support, minimization of feelings for a child seeking validation, frightened or frightening behaviour, or over-attending to emotion when a child needs limit-setting and a calm parental response. Longstanding misattunement in the caregiver-child relationship can lead to a child developing the belief that something is inherently wrong with them. The child, especially a particularly sensitive and emotionally attuned child, may come to feel that his or her emotions are inappropriate, that emotional expression and vulnerability are unacceptable, and that others cannot be depended upon for support when needed.

In this way, the parent's representation (or "internal working model") of relationships can be passed on to the current parent-child dyad. In fact, there is now substantial evidence to suggest that patterns of attachment are transmitted quite reliably across generations (e.g., Crawford & Benoit, 2009). Parents with a dismissing style are much more likely to have insecure children, particularly with an avoidant attachment style (van IJzendoorn, 1995), and these children will be at a greater risk of having a dismissive attachment style themselves as parents. This is important because the detrimental long-term effects of insecure attachment on later cognitive, psychological, and social functioning and health are well established (e.g., Malekpour, 2007; Perry, Pollard, Blakley, Baker, & Vigilante, 1995; Wartner, Grossman, Fremmer-Bombik, & Suess, 1994).

In order to understand the parent with a dismissing attachment style, it is important for us to recognize that the way parents respond to their children stem from their own childhood experiences (see Figure 6.1). A history of

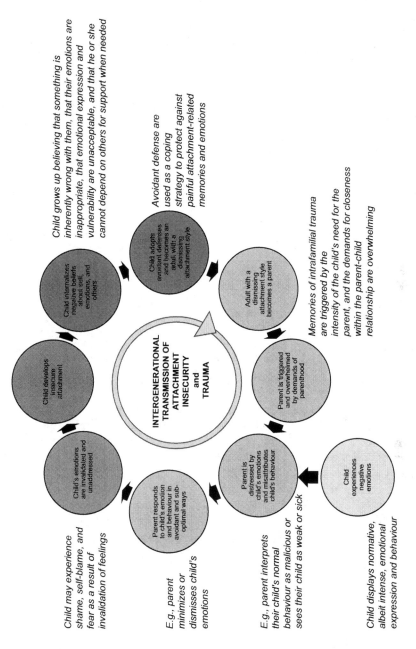

Figure 6.1 Intergenerational Transmission of Attachment and Insecurity

intrafamilial trauma can distort parents' interpretations of their child's behaviour. This misinterpretation, meant to protect them from painful re-experiencing of their own trauma, can have the unwanted effect of blocking them from noticing and attending to their child's emotional needs. It is also important for us to understand that parents with a dismissing style rely on deactivating strategies to protect themselves from a past that is too painful to acknowledge.

To empower parents to become the primary agent of change in their child's mental health and recovery, we need to prioritize the therapeutic relationship and create a supportive and safe space. It is in this safe space that parents' defences[1] can be both validated and challenged, and parents can begin to express their feelings in relation to their own lived trauma or unmet needs (Foroughe & Muller, 2012; Muller, 2010). This is often the first time these parents make themselves vulnerable and begin to restructure their fears of emotion and emotion expression.

We must also be mindful not to over-identify with either the parent or child. Therapists working primarily with children sometimes over-identify with the child, which can come across to the parent as taking sides or blaming the parent. Therapists can use blaming language when speaking about the difficulties the child is having, or speak about the child's challenges in a way that places all of the responsibility on the parent. Therapists can also speak about the child's difficulties in a way that only focuses on the child's experience, not attending to what the parent has been through or how he or she feels. This may leave the parent feeling ignored, condescended to, and blamed. In addition to negatively impacting the parent's sense of self-efficacy and intensifying feelings of guilt and shame, our attempts at emphasizing the child's perspective, without validating and supporting the parent, can undermine the therapeutic relationship.

On the other hand, therapists who work primarily with adults sometimes over-identify with the parent, further pathologizing or blaming the child by passively accepting the parent's condemnation of the child's behaviour or emotional expression without understanding the child's perspectives and needs. In doing so, the therapist may neglect to recognize and directly address a parent's own trauma history and deactivating strategies, in essence colluding with the parent's avoidance of attachment related memories, thoughts, and emotions. Instead, we can support the parent to access, explore, and heal their deeply buried emotional wounds—within the holding environment of the therapeutic relationship—so that they may move past their blocks to effectively support their child's mental health and recovery. As Fraiberg, Adelson, and Shapiro (1975) so simply and elegantly stated: "When (the) mother's own cries are heard, she will hear her child's cries" (p. 396).

Identifying Avoidance: Common Deactivating Strategies

Bowlby viewed attachment behaviour as biologically based and motivated by the need to maintain closeness with caregivers, especially during times of real or perceived danger (Bowlby, 1982, 1988; Bretherton, 1992). From this perspective, we can see how avoidant strategies are adaptive for parents with a trauma history (Freyd, 1996, 2001; Muller, 2009, 2010). Early in life, deactivation allows the child to stay physically close to their caregiver, who they depend upon for survival, despite a lack of emotional care and responsiveness. Later in life, avoidance allows the parent to disengage from the painful feelings and traumatic memories experienced with their own caregivers. This helps them protect their view of their own parents or caregivers and maintain a feeling of safety. However, when individuals continue to use avoidant strategies as adolescents and adults, these strategies can undermine new relationships and lead to considerable individual and interpersonal problems (Daniel, 2006; Edelstein & Shaver, 2004; Muller, 2010). In an attempt to continue to protect themselves from emotional danger, these strategies can interfere with the relationship with their children, despite a parent's best intentions.

How can we spot avoidance in therapy? To illustrate the defensive interpersonal patterns, we will return now to the case of Jennifer and her baby, Daniella. As part of the family's clinical assessment, Jennifer completed the Adult Attachment Interview (AAI; George, Kaplan, & Main, 1985)—a semi-structured assessment of individuals' mental representations of attachment (i.e., "internal working models"). During the AAI, parents are asked to recall childhood memories of their relationship with their primary caregivers and reflect on how these early experiences may have impacted their adult personality and behaviour. When asked about her early attachment experiences, Jennifer described her relationship with her parents using generalized and sometimes idealized terms (e.g., using words like "normal" and "wonderful" when talking about both parents). Yet, she was unable to recall specific memories relating to the terms she had chosen, often insisting on a lack of memory (e.g., saying "I don't remember") or providing very general responses. For example, when asked to share a specific incident or memory she had that would shed light on how her relationship with her mother was "supportive" (a word she had chosen earlier), she replied: "She was just ... always there, you know ... because she was a stay-at-home mom."

Additionally, although she alluded to some emotional neglect and physical abuse by both her parents when asked specifically about discipline during childhood, she minimized the impact or importance of this experience when probed further. Using a very matter-of-fact tone, she stated that her parents' use of severe physical punishment had no impact on her as a child or adult. She also described her experiences with discipline in childhood as "no big deal" and "normal, for the time." When asked specifically about any traumatic experiences, she denied having had any, again stating that everything was "really normal" in her family of origin, and then she asked to move onto the next question.

Later in therapy, and over the span of several sessions and with the attuned support of the therapist, Jennifer slowly began to uncover previously buried memories of her painful childhood experiences, recounting a history of severe physical and emotional abuse. At first, she continued to minimize the impact these experiences had on her. She distanced herself from her emotional pain by talking about her memories in a very intellectualized way (e.g., by focusing on non-relational aspects of the memory, like how the family car broke down and was expensive to fix) and using distancing language or generalizations such as "kids back then just respected their parents." Sometimes, there was a mismatch between the sad and often scary stories she would share in session and her own affect as she told these stories. For example, she laughed while recounting a time she had been severely beaten by her father with a leather belt after she had broken a glass at the dinner table.

Often, parents with a dismissing style can use deactivation to stave off attachment-related emotions and bury painful memories of early relationships with their caregivers. They tend to describe their early relationships in inconsistent, imbalanced ways, minimizing the painful feelings associated with attachment experiences or denying the impact of these experiences on their development. When asked, these clients struggle to remember or share specific childhood memories. Then, when they do begin to reveal their traumatic memories in therapy, they may normalize these negative experiences and maintain their self-perception and portrayal as strong, capable, and independent people. Table 6.1 summarizes some of the common defensive strategies we see in our work with this group of clients. Each of these defences protects the client from intense psychological pain in some way (e.g., by masking their fear of trusting others or their intense vulnerability, or by burying the fact that they are terrified of having their deep desire to be loved unmet by those around them). As therapists, ask ourselves: "What need might the defensive strategy meet for my client?" Then, with a genuine curiosity, we can invite the client to reflect on and make meaning of what is going on for them.

Table 6.1 Common Defensive Strategies (Parent Blocks or Protections in EFFT)

Defence	The Client in Therapy
Defensive exclusion of painful memories	• Uses general terms to describe attachment relationships • Struggles to recall specific childhood events, insisting on a lack of memory EXAMPLE: *Responds with "I don't remember" or "nothing comes to mind really" when asked about early attachment relationships*
Minimization	• Downplays the emotional significance, long-term impact, and negative effect or severity of trauma and attachment-related experiences • Attempts to see and portray experiences as "normal" EXAMPLE: *"The way my parents disciplined us was pretty normal . . . I mean . . . for the time . . . and anyway, it really wasn't a big deal"*
Positive ending	• A form of minimization • Ends a negative story positively and is unaware of the incoherence of the overall story EXAMPLE: *Stories of abuse or neglect may be positively wrapped up with "It was good because I learned how to be strong and take care of myself"*

Defence	The Client in Therapy
Idealization	• Describes one or both parents in extremely positive terms that are not consistent with the specific events or memories described • It's not uncommon for the abusive or emotionally absent parent to be idealized EXAMPLE: *A mom, who just moments earlier, was described as violent and depressed, later in the AAI is, out of nowhere, described in this way: "Yeah, mom was a pretty impressive lady . . . you know . . . putting up with the crap he threw her way"*
Intellectualization and talking around feelings	• Diverts attention from emotions by focusing instead on cognitive aspects of experiences, non-attachment related themes, or activities EXAMPLE: *May focus on or altogether change the topic to non-threatening issues, such as financial or legal difficulties* OR *May throw themselves into their work so intensely that it is at the expense of romantic relationships*
Self-perception as self-reliant, independent, strong, and normal	• Help-rejecting and defensive • Struggles to acknowledging the need for help, or may seek help for symptoms (e.g., difficulties sleeping or concentrating at work) EXAMPLE: *The client may distance or isolate themselves rather than seek support when dealing with stressful situations*
Distancing language	• Uses words or general phrases to distance themselves from attachment-related content EXAMPLE: *A client, describing her reaction to her father's violent outbursts, suddenly distances herself by switching to the pronoun "you": "You just knew not to get in his way"*

Intervention Strategies in Practice: A Case Example

Rose,[2] a 34-year-old mother of three young boys, started therapy because she was concerned by her two older children's behavioural issues, including toileting problems, emotional dysregulation, attentional difficulties, and severe temper tantrums. Over the course of a year in therapy, she gradually disclosed a complex trauma history involving severe childhood bullying, sexual assault, physical and emotional abuse by her father, the loss of several late-term pregnancies, and poverty. It quickly became apparent that Rose had developed a dismissing attachment style as a way of coping with these incredibly difficult experiences. She relied heavily on deactivating strategies to minimize and altogether avoid difficult emotions, protecting herself from her own painful feelings as well as the emotions of her three young children. Early in the therapy process, Rose spoke often of feeling "disconnected" from her two older boys and would express annoyance when her children experienced any type of intense emotion. When asked to reflect on what her children might be feeling, she became impatient and exasperated.

In an early therapy session, Rose described an episode where her two sons Jeremy (7 years old) and Jacob (5 years old) had been fighting over a toy:

Rose: Jeremy finally just grabbed his stuffy from Jacob, and Jacob just fell down and burst into tears. So dramatic. (rolls her eyes and sighs)
Therapist: Mmm. (nodding)
Rose: So he comes over to me crying and sobbing, looking ... I don't know ... for sympathy I guess (laughs).
Therapist: Mmm, he was looking for sympathy.
Rose: (laughs again) Yeah, but I just told him to stop it. He can't just cry every time he doesn't get his way. Crying just makes you look silly.
Therapist: You don't want him to look silly.
Rose: Right, I'm not going to coddle him. I mean I know he's 5, but kids are so coddled. How do you raise strong kids if you let them cry all the time?
Therapist: Mmm, so if you let them cry they can't be strong.
Rose: Yeah, you need to teach them to be strong right from the start. Can't be weak.

Notice Rose's minimization of her 5-year-old's emotions and the irritation his vulnerable feelings caused her. She also directly equated emotional expression with weakness. Recognizing that Rose's apparent intolerance of her child's emotions could stem from her own childhood experiences, the therapist explored this question with her directly.

Therapist: Is there a time in your childhood where you remember being told to stop crying and to be strong?
Rose: (laughs) Of course! Like when Dad's brother died. Dad always said: 'You can have one day to cry. That's it. Then you have to buck up and move on with life.' (laughs) People die. Plain and simple. Crying isn't going to change that for you. (laughs)

In the exchange above, Rose's nonverbal and para-verbal behaviour was discordant with the story she was telling. For example, while talking about the death of her uncle and her crying 5-year-old, her story was punctuated with laughter and eye rolling. She used distancing language when asked about her own emotions, referring to herself using the pronoun "you": "*You* have to buck up and move on with life" and "Crying isn't going to change that for *you*." Here, the therapist invited Rose to connect the situation with her sons to her own childhood experiences. In response, Rose revealed a history of early emotion-minimization by her own father. Although she was able to speak about a time when she tried to express emotion and was shut down, her story focused entirely on her father's advice to "buck up and stay strong." That is, instead of talking about her feelings, her response to the therapist avoided her own internal experience entirely. As you can see, in the excerpt above, Rose showed several different ways that a client might avoid emotion within the context of a therapy session as a form of self-protection.

Shining a Spotlight on Emotion

Because distancing oneself from painful emotion is the hallmark of avoidant attachment, and because this has negative consequences for parenting and close relationships, it is important that the therapist identify and empathize with the parent's vulnerabilities. McCullough and colleagues used the term "affect phobia" to characterize the difficulty many have with their own internal experience. Helping a parent with a dismissing attachment style learn to tolerate and manage emotions is important because they can find it so painful or dangerous to connect with and mentalize their child's vulnerable feelings.

In order to help parents, we first must notice the subtle cues that reveal their struggle: answering questions in a way that skims over or dances around emotional material; body language and behaviour that do not match the negative content of their stories; and answering questions about their feelings in a way that focuses on facts or action, or intellectualizes their experience. As therapists, it is helpful to purposefully and thoughtfully target affect when working with these parents. Using the safe context of the therapeutic relationship, we must: 1) bring the client back to emotion, 2) notice disconnect between content and affect, 3) have the client connect to different feelings currently in the room and in their body, 4) notice and address when a client uses distancing, and 5) connect stories and experiences by recognizing common re-emerging emotional threads.

As with all psychotherapies, the importance of establishing a safe and secure working relationship cannot be overstated. When working with parents with a dismissing style, we need to foster a sense of "emotional safety" by taking a curious and non-judgmental stance when thinking about and working with emotions. These clients rarely acknowledge painful feelings on their own. As therapists, one of the first things we can do is notice emotions in a way that doesn't judge or place value on one over the other. It is important that the parent feels like we accept and value all emotions as they are. This non-judgmental stance models for them that feelings are acceptable and normalizes emotional expression.

In the session below, Rose had been coming to therapy for about six weeks. She talked about an incident where she found out her husband had been secretly driving a female co-worker to work every day for the last six months. She only discovered this because the female co-worker had left a pair of women's gloves in the family mini-van. Rose found them and confronted her husband. At this point in therapy, Rose's tendency to avoid emotion was already clear from earlier sessions, so her therapist could now draw Rose's attention back to her feelings throughout sessions as a way of increasing awareness of her internal experience.

Rose: (laughs) So I held up the gloves and knew right away they didn't belong to me or my kids . . . and they definitely didn't belong to him.
Therapist: You knew they belonged to someone else.
Rose: (laughs) Oh yeah. So I sort of threw them at him and was like 'I don't know whose these are, but they probably want them back.' You should have seen the look on his face. He started mumbling about some coworker he was driving to work. But, whatever, it's not like I care. I just don't understand why he wouldn't tell me in the first place. Like what a stupid thing to lie about.
Therapist: I see. (nods)
Rose: I don't really care. I just don't understand the point of him hiding it.

Here we see Rose tried to dance around tough emotions she might have been experiencing, first by dismissing that any feelings existed and by minimizing what happened, telling the therapist she "didn't really care."

Therapist: I noticed you laughed when you talked about finding the gloves, but the story you told me doesn't sound like it was really funny for you. I wonder what was going on for you when you laughed?

The therapist pointed out the discrepancy between the material in the story Rose was telling and her laughter. That is, the therapist drew attention to the difference between the story content and her affect. Then, with a tone of genuine curiosity, the therapist invited Rose to reflect on what was going on for her as she retold the story.

Rose: (laughs again) I mean . . . I don't know . . . Okay yeah, I guess it wasn't funny . . . no . . . I just . . . It wasn't that big a deal. I just laugh sometimes I guess . . . I don't know . . . I guess it's a coping mechanism (laughs).
Therapist: Mmhmm . . . Okay, and that's normal to try to avoid feeling something by laughing it off. It can be so much easier for us to laugh instead of feel anger or hurt. I wonder if maybe you can take me back to the exact moment that you found the gloves. What were the feelings you experienced when you saw them lying there?

The therapist validated how difficult it was for Rose to identify her feelings, normalizing Rose's struggle. Still, the therapist gently encouraged Rose to push through, think back, and re-experience the memory to help her connect to what she might have been feeling when she first found the gloves.

Rose: Uhm . . . well . . . (pause 4 sec) I remember thinking 'what the hell?'

Therapist: That's a great example of a thought but what about what you were feeling?

When pushed further for a feeling, Rose avoided her psychological pain by talking about a thought she had instead of an emotion. This is a common protective strategy among clients with a dismissing style. In response, the therapist gently redirected Rose back to the task of identifying the *emotion* rather than the *thought*.

Rose: Uhm ... I don't ... (rolls eyes) ... (sighs)
Therapist: I'm noticing that it's really tough for you to speak about how you were feeling in that moment. I'm wondering if you could tell me what emotions you are feeling right now when I ask you to try this?

Because Rose struggled to reimagine her feelings from the past, she was asked by her therapist to try and identify what she was feeling in session, at that very moment.

Rose: (sighs) ... Irritation I guess.
Therapist: Okay that's a good one to start with, what does the irritation feel like? Like what sensations in your body are you feeling when you feel irritation, and where?

Here, Rose was asked to explore bodily sensations as a way of helping her tap into her felt emotions. This served to ground her as well as help her become mindful of what she was experiencing.

Rose: Uhm ... like tingling I guess ... in my head ... (pause 3 sec) ... and tightness in my face and hands.
Therapist: Mmhmm, that's great, I can really picture what you're feeling when you describe it that way. Since we have already talked about the feeling of 'irritation,' when you think back to finding those gloves, do you remember any irritation?
Rose: Yeah ... I guess ... mmm ...
Therapist: Mmhmm.
Rose: Well like ... I don't know ... uhm ... (pause 4 sec) ... uhm ... (pause 5 sec)
Therapist: This is hard for you. It's so tough for you to think back to those uncomfortable feelings. That's okay, let's just slow it down and really take a moment to think about this. Maybe you can try describing to me the way your body felt when you found the gloves? What sensations did you remember noticing?
Rose: Well ... I felt the tingling like I mentioned before ... but there was also this, like, boulder, that like, dropped into my stomach, (pause 3 sec) ... making me sick.

Therapist: Mmm, you started feeling sick.
Rose: Sort of ... uhh ...
Therapist: (nods)
Rose: Uhm ... My heart was also beating really fast, and my hands were sweaty. I remember that because I was holding the gloves and they got sweaty too.
Therapist: That sounds so difficult for you, it sounds like finding the gloves almost made you sick.
Rose: I guess I started panicking ... It sounds stupid when I say it out loud, but like in that moment, I kinda panicked that he was going to leave me and the kids.

Gently, and persistently, the therapist continued to encourage Rose to connect with her emotions. She was challenged to stay with the emotion and the bodily sensations they created. She was allowed to struggle a bit with what was being asked of her, and her therapist sat with her through that struggle. Overall, Rose's awareness was continually being drawn back to her emotions and internal experiences, and she was coached to begin thinking about experiences that she was having with her child through an emotion-focused lens.

Debriefing an Emotional Session

When parents start tackling their emotions within a session, they inevitably experience moments of vulnerability. This, especially in a parent who has a trauma history, can lead to feelings of fear, shame, guilt, and disgust. Emotion avoidance serves to protect the parent from having to experience these painful feelings. Avoidance also protects them from the danger of exposing these emotions to another person. Having another person witness their emotions can feel very frightening.

It can be helpful to debrief an emotionally evocative session and "unpack" what that experience of being vulnerable was like for the parent. As therapists, we can take the last 10 to 15 minutes of an emotional session to ask questions about what it was like for the parent, to talk about their feelings, and perhaps to express emotion in our presence and experience their feelings more openly. First, taking this time to debrief can help contain and regulate the individual so that they are able to ground themselves before leaving the session. Also, if the person has cried, for example, we can normalize the act of crying and validate their need to express their emotions in this way. We can ask questions like: "What was it like for you to (cry/be vulnerable/have a strong emotion) in front of me?"; "What part was most (or least) difficult?"; or "What effect has it had on your feelings toward me as your therapist?" By openly talking about a vulnerable act such as crying, we, as therapists, are also modelling for the client that we can "handle" their tears and expressions of strong feelings.

Debriefing allows us to explore what it was like for the parent to show emotion and gives them space to tell us about any shame, disgust, self-judgment, or any other number of secondary emotions they may have been experiencing. It also allows us to draw attention to the therapeutic relationship and use this relationship as a support for encouraging their emotional expression.

We can use the information discovered during debriefing to make connections between past and present experiences of intense emotion and past reactions they and others have had to similar emotions. This allows the parent to further understand their avoidance, recognize their own patterns, and make meaning of their experiences. Most importantly, debriefing a difficult session together means that the parent will not have to be hit with the aftermath alone—the processing of emotion is begun within the safety and support of the therapeutic relationship.

Directly Addressing Distancing Manoeuvres

Empathy and attunement, although necessary for a healthy alliance, can be destabilizing and threatening for parents with a dismissing style who avoid vulnerability. For a person with a history of interpersonal trauma, experiencing intimacy, trust, and empathy can run counter to past relational experiences. Feeling a therapist's empathy also means exposing their inner experience. There can be an underlying fear that the shame and disgust the individual feels about their own emotional expression will be noticed and shared by the therapist. Furthermore, establishing an empathic connection with a therapist can provoke a fear of dependency and rejection. The uncomfortable experience of vulnerability and of having their emotions witnessed invokes a drive to restore control.

To manage this fear of vulnerability, intimacy, and loss of control, individuals often engage in *distancing manoeuvres* (Muller, 2010) if they feel too close or too exposed. These manoeuvres serve to put at arm's-length a relationship that has grown too intimate, and to restore equilibrium. Distancing can take many different forms. The parent may dismiss or laugh off comments we make, "forget" to show up to the session, avoid eye contact, or take a phone call during the session. The person may forget to mention important things that are going on in their lives, or use the session time to share a litany of vague complaints. Distancing can also be observed in more subtle, behavioural ways. For example, the parent may keep her bag or purse on her lap, effectively creating a barrier between her and her therapist. As therapists, we work hard to build a sense of trust and closeness with our clients, yet a parent with a dismissing style may react to this closeness by pulling back and protecting themselves. Remember, this is because closeness can feel dangerous and threatening. The challenge for the therapist then is to resist the urge to pull back as well, or become intimidated by the parent's seemingly cold or unresponsive style.

Following a few sessions where a lot of emotion was brought into the room and experienced by both the therapist and client, Rose's therapist noticed a developing pattern of distancing. Rose had been attending therapy for 10 weeks and had two sessions in a row where she and her therapist explored some very painful moments of rejection and emotional trauma during her childhood. These sessions were hard for Rose because, as she talked about in the debriefing, she hated crying in front of her therapist and was ashamed of "being weak." She expressed her worry that the therapist would get "sick of her and her tears."

The week following these two very emotionally intimate sessions, Rose brought her 9-month-old son with her to therapy. She mentioned that her mother, who usually babysat while she came to therapy, had some errands to run, and couldn't take the child that day. Her therapist didn't think much of this at the time and didn't say anything. Rose and her family had very limited social and financial resources so she understood Rose being unable to find someone to babysit on short notice. The therapist did, however, notice that during that session the conversation remained focused on "safe" topics. Also, much of Rose's attention throughout the hour was diverted to the baby, and she avoided talking about any material that was emotionally evocative for her. At the time, the therapist was also distracted by the baby who was very active and fussy (but adorable!). After the session, the therapist remembered thinking the meeting felt disjointed, superficial, and unproductive.

The next few sessions Rose did not bring her baby, and over the course of three weeks, they delved into a very poignant memory of her being sexually assaulted in the schoolyard by an older student. Rose's therapist spent a lot of time debriefing at the end of these sessions because of their difficult emotional content. At the end of the third session, Rose said tearfully that the last time she spoke about this incident, her father beat her for "leading the boy on." She admitted feelings of guilt, shame, and responsibility for what happened to her. She indeed asked the therapist at one point if, in her "professional opinion," she had "made" the boy assault her.

The very next session, after discussing these painful feelings of shame, Rose, again, brought her baby with her. As it was the second time Rose had done this, the therapist began to wonder if this was a pattern, and what this pattern might be about. But, captivating as babies are, the two spent much of the session distracted by the little one and his attempts to stand up and toddle about. Again, only afterward, while writing her session notes, the therapist was struck by how unproductive the meeting felt.

After a third occurrence of Rose bringing the baby following an emotional session, Rose's therapist brought the issue to supervision. It became clear that, after a particularly evocative meeting, Rose would bring in the baby, and the session would feel shallow and aimless. She would "regroup" or put distance in the therapeutic relationship because of how exposing it was to explore the previous session's material. She was, quite literally, using the baby as a security blanket, with the added benefit of both the therapist and Rose getting easily distracted by the infant. And so, the next time Rose repeated the pattern, the therapist brought it up in session:

Therapist: So, we've been working together for a while now and I've begun to notice a pattern and I'm wondering if you've noticed it at all?
Rose: What's that?
Therapist: Well, I've noticed that every time we have a particularly tough session, the next session you will bring in James (her baby).
Rose: ... Hmm ... uhm ... I hadn't really thought about it to be honest.
Therapist: Okay, and that's okay. I also notice that when you do bring in James, we don't talk about much, and I feel a little disconnected from you. Like the session feels like we remain mostly on surface level stuff and avoid a lot of the tougher issues. I'm wondering if you've noticed this also?
Rose: Uh ... yeah ... I mean I guess ... uhh ...
Therapist: Mhm.
Rose: Well I mean ... I guess I never thought about it before. It's not like it's conscious, you know?
Therapist: Hmm okay, yeah. I see. We don't always ask ourselves our reasons for doing every little thing. I think, though, it might really be important to think about this and what it might mean about what you are feeling.
Rose: I guess, okay.
Therapist: I'm wondering, if you can try to describe to me what you were feeling as you were getting ready to come in today after we had such an emotional session last week?

Just as directly addressing emotions is important, it is equally important to directly address when a parent attempts to distance themselves from us. Distancing manoeuvres are inevitable, they are part-and-parcel of the work; and if we can recognize them for what they are, a protection against the anticipated pain of closeness and intimacy, they can be an opportunity for therapeutic growth. Bringing these instances into awareness helps parents with a dismissing style understand what emotions are particularly difficult for them to experience, and their "go-to" strategies for avoiding them. Helping them recognize these patterns allows them to develop a greater awareness of their inner experience. As clients become more self-aware, they start self-correcting. Rose became very good at noticing and "snitching on herself" (as she light heartedly labelled it) when she used humour to dismiss or avoid a strong emotion. She would do something like make a joke while talking about a family member's death, and then stop herself and say, "I guess that's me avoiding again." She and her therapist could then discuss what it was she was avoiding and what she was feeling when she made the joke.

Conclusion

When working with parents with a dismissing style, it is important that the therapist facilitate understanding of the parent's own emotions and emotional history, so that they can better understand their experience of the child. In shining a spotlight on emotion from early on in therapy, the therapist can strive to: always bring the client back to their emotional experience; notice disconnect in what a parent is saying and their affect as they say it; build the parent's awareness of the physical sensations that accompany their emotions; help the client recognize re-emerging emotional themes; address it directly (and gently) when a client uses distancing; and debrief toward the end of sessions in which there was a high level of emotionality, whether overtly expressed or subtly shown through the parent's cues. In doing so, we can partner with parents to help them move away from dismissing and avoidant coping mechanisms, recognize their own emotional needs including historically unmet needs, and be able to respond to the emotional needs of their child.

Dos and Don'ts for Working With Dismissing Attachment (Avoidance) in Trauma

DO

- Pay attention to your client's nonverbal (e.g., body shifts and posture, facial expressions, etc.) and para-verbal (e.g., pace, pitch, tone of speech, etc.) cues, noticing emotions that come up in therapy.
- With a tone of genuine curiosity, start working with emotions by asking the client to pay attention to how their *body* feels in connection with their experiences. Then, help your client link those bodily sensations to feelings.
- Help the client make connections between past and present emotional themes by drawing attention to patterns that have come up in therapy and inviting him or her to reflect on and make meaning of those patterns.
- Be on the lookout for client avoidance (HINT: keep in mind the defensive strategies described earlier in this chapter). Recognize avoidance as your client's attempt to protect themselves from emotional pain, and see it as a therapeutic opportunity to address your client's defences directly. For example:
    - Notice when the client disconnects from the emotional thread in session (e.g., through minimization or intellectualized speech) and bring the client back to the affect
    - Notice and reflect on any discrepancies between expressed emotions and nonverbal behaviours

- Invite your client to reflect on similarities and differences between their current struggles and their childhood experiences
- Notice and address any emotions that arise for the client in relation to you. Use these moments as a point of entry—ask your client to reflect on what they were feeling toward you and how that experience might relate to how they feel about other current or past relationships.
- Be aware of how avoidance and distancing might make *you* feel (e.g., feelings of rejection, irritation, and anxiety are common) and act (e.g., Do you tend to back off when the client distances him or herself?).
- Debrief with the client after a difficult session or discussion: What was it like talking about the difficult memory/experience/emotion, etc.? What was it like for them to discuss with you any feelings they had about you, your therapeutic relationship, or the therapy process generally?

DON'T

- Collude with client avoidant strategies, e.g., neglecting to directly address attachment-related experiences, memories, or emotions by:
    - Ignoring discrepancies between *what* your client says and *how* he or she says it (e.g., when a client laughs while recounting a sad or scary memory)
    - Failing to reconnect the session and your client to emotions when he or she goes "offline"
    - Quickly moving on to non-relational content or keeping your client's processing at an intellectual level when your client distances him or herself
- Undervalue the therapeutic relationship as a vehicle for discussing and exploring past and present emotional experiences.
- Underestimate the power of empathy—note, however, that it can trigger client fear and avoidance of vulnerability (e.g., anxiety around trusting and/or relying on others, a fear of appearing weak).
- Tune out your own feelings in the treatment. This can happen when we:
    - Neglect to recognize how and when we get pulled into the client's avoidance
    - Fail to reflect on our emotional and behavioural responses to the client, and what those responses might say about us

Notes

1 In EFFT, "defences" are referred to as "fears and blocks."
2 All identifying information, including the client's name, has been changed. The second author (SR) was the therapist in Rose's case example.

References

Bartholomew, K., & Horowitz, L. M. (1991). Attachment styles among young adults: A test of a four-category model. *Journal of Personality and Social Psychology, 61*(2), 226–244. doi:10.1037/0022-3514.61.2.226

Bowlby, J. (1982). *Attachment and loss, Vol. 1. Attachment* (2nd ed.). New York, NY: Basic Books.

Bowlby, J. (1988). *A secure base: Parent-child attachment and healthy human development.* New York, NY: US Basic Books.

Bretherton, I. (1992). The origins of attachment theory: John Bowlby and Mary Ainsworth. *Developmental Psychology, 28*(5), 759–775. doi:10.1037/0012-1649.28.5.759

Chu, J. A. (1998). *Rebuilding shattered lies: The responsible treatment of complex post-traumatic and dissociative disorders.* New York, NY: Wiley.

Crawford, A., & Benoit, D. (2009). Caregivers' disrupted representations of the unborn child predict later infant-caregiver disorganized attachment and disrupted interactions. *Infant Mental Health Journal, 30*(2), 124–144. doi:10.1002/imhj.20207

Crowell, J. A., & Feldman, S. S. (1988). Mothers' internal models of relationships and children's behavioral and developmental status: A study of mother-child interaction. *Child Development, 59*(5), 1273–1285. doi:10.2307/1130490

Dalenberg, C. J. (2000). *Counter transference and the treatment of trauma.* Washington, DC: American Psychological Association. doi:10.1037/10380-000

Daniel, S. I. F. (2006). Adult attachment patterns and individual psychotherapy: A review. *Clinical Psychology Review, 26*(8), 968–984. doi:10.1016/j.cpr.2006.02.001

Davies, J. M., & Frawley, M. G. (1994). *Treating the adult survivor of childhood sexual abuse: A psychoanalytic perspective.* New York, NY: Basic Books.

Dozier, M., & Kobak, R. R. (1992). Psychophysiology in adolescent attachment interviews: Convergent evidence for dismissing strategies. *Child Development, 63*, 1473–1480. doi:10.2307/1131569

Eagle, M. N. (2006). Attachment, psychotherapy, and assessment: A commentary. *Journal of Consulting and Clinical Psychology, 74*(6), 1086–1097. doi:10.1037/0022-006X.74.6.1086

Edelstein, R. S., & Gillath, O. (2008). Avoiding interference: Adult attachment and emotional processing biases. *Personality and Social Psychology Bulletin, 34*(2), 171–181. doi:10.1177/0146167207310024

Edelstein, R. S., & Shaver, P. R. (2004). Avoidant attachment: Exploration of an oxymoron. In D. J. Mashek & A. P. Aron (Eds.), *Handbook of closeness and intimacy; handbook of closeness and intimacy* (pp. 397–412, Chapter x, 454 Pages). Mahwah, NJ: Lawrence Erlbaum Associates.

Foroughe, M. F., & Muller, R. T. (2012). Dismissing (avoidant) attachment and trauma in dyadic parent-child psychotherapy. *Psychological Trauma: Theory, Research, Practice, and Policy, 4*(2), 229–236. doi:10.1037/a0023061

Foroughe, M. F., & Muller, R. T. (2014). Attachment-based intervention strategies in family therapy with survivors of intra-familial trauma: A case study. *Journal of Family Violence, 29*(5), 539–548. doi:10.1007/s10896-014-9607-4

Fraiberg, S., Adelson, E., & Shapiro, V. (1975). Ghosts in the nursery: A psychoanalytic approach to the problems of impaired infant-mother relationships. *Journal of American Academy of Child Psychiatry, 14*, 387–421.

Freyd, J. J. (1996). *Betrayal trauma: The logic of forgetting childhood abuse.* Cambridge, MA: Harvard University Press.

Freyd, J. J. (2001). Memory and dimensions of trauma: Terror may be "all-too-well remembered" and betrayal buried. In J. R. Conte (Ed.), *Critical issues in child sexual abuse: Historical, legal, and psychological perspectives* (pp. 139–173). Thousand Oaks, CA: Sage.

George, C., Kaplan, N., & Main, M. (1985). *Adult attachment interview*. Unpublished manuscript, University of California, Berkeley, CA.

Hesse, E., & Main, M. (2006). Frightened, threatening, and dissociative parental behavior in low-risk samples: Description, discussion, and interpretations. *Development and Psychopathology, 18*(2), 309–343. doi:10.1017/S0954579406060172

Konanur, S., Muller, R. T., Cinamon, J. S., Thornback, K., & Zorzella, K. P. M. (2015). Effectiveness of trauma-focused cognitive behavioral therapy in a community-based program. *Child Abuse & Neglect, 50*, 159–170. doi:10.1016/j.chiabu.2015.07.013

Main, M., & Hesse, E. (1990). Parents' unresolved traumatic experiences are related to infant disorganized attachment status: Is frightened and/or frightening parental behavior the linking mechanism? In M. Greenberg, D. Cicchetti, & E. M. Cummings (Eds.), *Attachment in the preschool years: Theory, research and intervention* (pp. 161–184). Chicago: University of Chicago Press.

Malekpour, M. (2007). Effects of attachment on early and later development. *British Journal of Developmental Disabilities, 53*(105), 81–95. doi:10.1179/096979507799103360

Muller, R. T. (2009). Trauma and dismissing (avoidant) attachment: Intervention strategies in Individual psychotherapy. *Psychotherapy: Theory, Research, Practice, Training, 46*(1), 68–81. doi:10.1037/a0015135

Muller, R. T. (2010). *Trauma and the avoidant client: Attachment-based strategies for healing*. New York, NY: W.W. Norton.

Muller, R. T. (in press). *Trauma and the struggle to open up: From avoidance to recovery and growth*. New York, NY: W.W. Norton.

Muller, R. T., & Rosenkranz, S. E. (2009). Attachment and treatment response among adults in inpatient treatment for posttraumatic stress disorder. *Psychotherapy: Theory, Research, Practice, Training, 46*(1), 82–96. doi:10.1037/a0015137

Pearlman, L. A., & Courtois, C. A. (2005). Clinical applications of the attachment framework: Relational treatment of complex trauma. *Journal of Traumatic Stress, 18*(5), 449–459. doi:10.1002/jts.20052

Pearlman, L. A., & Saakvitne, K. W. (1995). *Trauma and the therapist: Counter transference and vicarious traumatization in psychotherapy with incest survivors*. New York, NY: W W Norton & Co.

Perry, B. D., Pollard, R. A., Blakley, T. L., Baker, W. L., & Vigilante, D. (1995). Childhood trauma, the neurobiology of adaptation, and "use-dependent" development of the brain: How "states" become "traits." *Infant Mental Health Journal, 16*(4), 271–291.

van IJzendoorn, M. H. (1995). Adult attachment representations, parental responsiveness, and infant attachment: A meta-analysis on the predictive validity of the adult attachment interview. *Psychological Bulletin, 117*(3), 387–403. doi:10.1037/0033-2909.117.3.387

Wartner, U. G., Grossmann, K., Fremmer-Bombik, E., & Suess, G. (1994). Attachment patterns at age six in south Germany: Predictability from infancy and implications for preschool behavior. *Child Development, 65*(4), 1014–1027. doi:10.2307/1131301

Zorzella, K. P. M., Rependa, S. L., & Muller, R. T. (2017). Therapeutic alliance over the course of child trauma and therapy from three different perspectives. *Child Abuse & Neglect, 67*, 147–156.

7 Practical Resources

Mirisse Foroughe, Joanne Dolhanty, and Adèle Lafrance

Session Note: Emotion Focused Family Therapy— Carer Model

Date: _____ Name: _____
Session number: _____ Session length: _____
Client Identification: _____

EFFT—General:

- Review the four foci of treatment (EC, RC, RR, PB) and provide rationale for EFFT (including website link)
- Review causes of mental health issues and emphasize importance of carer involvement
- Address the stress on the couple relationship if relevant and recommend *Hold Me Tight* by Sue Johnson
- Review the dynamics common to split-parents, if relevant, and the ways in which each parent can contribute to breaking the negative cycles

Recovery Coaching:

- Frame the work as Advanced Caregiving skills
- Identify carer concerns related to their loved one's symptoms (anxiety, depression, ED, cutting, etc.)
- Reframe behaviours/symptoms as a way to manage or avoid painful emotions
- Assess carers' self-efficacy in managing these behaviours; introduce the concept of carer blocks ("it's not about the skills")
- Provide carers with practical skills to support their loved one's behaviours if necessary (e.g., review risk assessments, develop safety plans and teach carers how to talk about suicidal ideation, for example)
- RC role-play/experiential practice

Additional Notes: _____
_____
_____

Emotion Coaching:

- Frame the work as Advanced Caregiving skills
- Introduce concept of superfeeler
- Reframe loved one's symptoms as ways to avoid emotional pain
- Review steps of Emotion Coaching
- Reframe miscues as attempts to protect loved one/carer relationships
- EC role-play/experiential practice

Copyright material from Mirisse Foroughe, 2018, *Emotion Focused Family Therapy with Children and Caregivers*, Routledge

Additional Notes: _____
_____
_____
_____

Relationship Repair:

- Frame the work as Advanced Caregiving skills
- Review the rationale for Relationship Repair and support carer to identify an injury if appropriate
- Review steps of RR
- Review the potential outcomes of RR (blast, denial, silence, etc.)
- Determine whether the carer feels prepared to present the apology and confidently manage their emotional response (may require another session to process any blocks which may arise)
- RR role-play/experiential practice

Additional Notes: _____
_____
_____
_____

Carer Blocks:

- Respond to carers' blocks and therapy-interfering behaviours using the skills of Emotion Coaching, with an emphasis on validation
- Normalize how current crisis can magnify caregiving styles and contribute to the development and maintenance of symptoms
- Review diagram of Therapy-Interfering Behaviours (and underlying emotions such as fear, shame, etc.)
- Review Animal Models (courtesy of Dr. Janet Treasure)
- Administer Caregiving Traps measure (identify relevant items and compare with partner if relevant)
- Administer Caregiving Dimensions measure (identify relevant items and compare with partner if relevant)
- Determine which blocks are interfering most with carers' ability to support their loved one in each of the EFFT domains
- Complete chair work specific to carer block

Additional Notes: _____
_____
_____

Plan for next session: _____

Copyright material from Mirisse Foroughe, 2018, *Emotion Focused Family Therapy with Children and Caregivers*, Routledge

EFFT Report: Parent Block—How To

Name of Parent _____ Date of Session _____
Parent is: Father/Mother   Re their: Daughter/Son   Age of Child _____
Parenting Dimensions Form Completed? Yes/No
More Sensitive to Abandon/Disrespect?

1. Brief Scenario:

One sentence to describe the context or situation of the block, e.g., father wants son to stop playing video games, can't get him to stop.

2. Marker:

What does the parent want to change or feel they should change but is not able or willing to do?
OR
What does the clinician see as problematic/needing change that the parent is not able or willing to do?

3. Voice/Brain Boss Command:

What does the parent tell themselves to keep doing, even though it is not working? To keep doing things the way they're doing them now? To keep themselves from changing their approach?

That is, to keep them *doing* something they *don't* want to do anymore *or* to *stop* themselves from doing what they *do* want to do. Generally, in categories such as:

- *Don't* set a boundary or limit, *don't* take responsibility, *don't* do Emotion Coaching, *don't* apologize
- *Do* keep criticizing/judging/reacting in the same old way
- *Don't* stop him from playing his game. Continue *not* to set limits and to get frustrated.

4. Parent's Threat to Self:

How does the parent scare or threaten themselves into continuing to do what is not working?
How does the self scare the self/How does the parent's "voice" scare them?

- "If you don't keep doing it this way . . ." What do they tell themselves will go badly?
  - If you get strict with him he will reject you and you will lose him, for example

Copyright material from Mirisse Foroughe, 2018, *Emotion Focused Family Therapy with Children and Caregivers*, Routledge

5. **Parent's Painful Feeling They Are Protecting Themselves From:**

   What is the deep feeling underlying the parent's scaring themselves?

   - You will feel so rejected/abandoned/sad/lonely

   What childhood memory did the parent use to remind themselves of that feeling, i.e., when they were abandoned/shamed?

   - For example, remember when you felt so abandoned and sad when your dad left?

6. **Child's Response:**

   What's the child's response on hearing the parent's plan?

   - Hurt/anger/relief/resignation?

   What's the child's feeling underlying the response?

7. **Parent's Response and Feeling:**

   Did shift occur?
   What prompted the shift?
   If not, what reinforced the block?
   What is the parent's plan going forward?
   How did the parent feel about the process? Any other observations from the process or debrief?

EFFT Processing Parent Block Practice Sheet

Step 1:

- Always start with the parent on your left in order to identify the marker. Once the marker for the parent block is identified, then . . .

Step 2: Other Chair—Enact the Block

Switch the parent to "other" chair *on the right*

- Instruct the parent to: "Be the part of you that convinces you . . ."
    - to not set limits, not to push the child, to continue to accommodate to the illness, to not to take responsibility for what the child is going through
- Really convince (scare) "yourself" that it would be a bad idea . . . "Because if you do, then . . ."
    - (Don't push her to go to school because if you do she will do something worse like run away. If you set limits you'll push him too far and he'll get more depressed and become suicidal, they will end up back in hospital.)
- Be specific about how it will be bad for them—as the parent
    - She will deteriorate, or worse—die. That it will be your fault and you won't be able to forgive yourself or she'll reject you and go live with her father, or won't speak to you again—push you out of her treatment all together.
- Tell yourself what to do instead—in other words, keep enacting the block (repeat of first instruction)
    - Just keep doing things the way you are now, e.g., allow her to run the household.
- Barter/negotiate, etc.
    - It's better to have a sick child than a dead child.

Switch

Step 3: Self Chair—Parent Reacts to the Block and Tells Child the Plan

- Ask the parent to picture their child in the other chair and tell them that they will continue to do as the block says and why.
    - "I'm too scared to stand up to you. I don't want to hurt you. I won't push you to eat."; "I feel really guilty but I am going to keep letting you stay home from school because I'm too afraid of the conflict."; "I feel relief when I blame the team and so I am going to keep doing that."

Switch

Copyright material from Mirisse Foroughe, 2018, *Emotion Focused Family Therapy with Children and Caregivers*, Routledge

Step 4: Other Chair—Be the Child and React

- Ask the parent: "As your child, what happens here?"
- If the child softens (e.g., cries, says they want/need their parent's help)—deepen by asking specifically why they want them to support them with recovery.
    - "You know me best, I need your help, I love you."
- If anger/resignation/relief—say if the child could speak what's underneath that anger, what would they say? ("Even though I don't always show it, I need you, I can't do this without you, I'm scared.")—Then deepen the softening, the longing, the love, and the need for the parent to take charge even when she opposes, etc.
    - (Most important part: "Tell her why you want her, why she is the most important to you, how much and how deeply you love her . . ."—this will help the parent to soften and "dig deep" for the next switch.)

Switch

Step 5: Self Chair—Parent Reacts to the Child

- Ask the parent: "What happens when you hear this?"
    - Do they feel a sense of responsibility, sadness, empowerment?
- Encourage the communication of love and compassion (deepen this as well).
- Encourage parent to tell child what they will do differently from now on—be specific.
    - I am going to follow the meal-plan set by the hospital; I am going to make sure I stay calm when we talk about your symptoms; I am going to be strong when you can't be.
- Support the parent to warn the child that it won't go perfectly but that they won't give up.
    - I know I might lose my temper, or make mistakes, but I am determined to keep going.

Switch

Step 6: Other Chair—Child Reacts to Parent's Apology/Revised Plan

- As the child, ask them to share how it feels to hear that (even if it evokes fear or doubt), encourage the expression of gratitude—help the "child" to express what's underneath the fear/doubt.

Copyright material from Mirisse Foroughe, 2018, *Emotion Focused Family Therapy with Children and Caregivers*, Routledge

- Thank you, I want to believe things can be different but they've not gone well before, I'm scared it will be too hard for you, or you will get angry with me but underneath—I feel relief—I really need you, I can't do this alone.

Switch

Step 7: Self Chair—Have Parent Connect With Therapist

- Ask the parent to tell you (the therapist) how it feels to hear this from the child

Debrief (End here)

EFFT Report: Clinician Block—Parent Involvement—How To

Name of Clinician _____ Date of Supervision Session _____

1. *Brief Scenario:*

One sentence to describe the context or situation of the block.

- Doesn't want to have angry father into session, for example.

2. *Marker:*

- What does the clinician want to change or feel they should change but is not able or willing to do?

OR

- What does the supervisor see as problematic/needing change that the clinician is not able or willing to do?

3. *Voice/Brain Boss Command:*

What does the clinician tell themselves to convince themselves not to involve the parent? To keep doing things the way they're doing them now? To keep themselves from changing their approach?

- Don't invite that parent into the therapy, for example.

4. *Clinician's Threat to Self:*

How does the clinician scare or threaten themselves into not involving the parent, i.e., how does the clinician's self scare the self/how does the clinician's "voice" scare them? What do they tell themselves will go badly?

- If you invite him in, he will get angry and you will feel vulnerable, for example.

5. *Clinician's Painful Feeling They Are Protecting Themselves From:*

What is the deep feeling underlying the clinician's scaring themselves?

- You will feel vulnerable and scared and embarrassed for feeling that.

What childhood memory did the clinician use to remind themselves of that feeling, i.e., when they were vulnerable/abandoned/shamed?

- Remember when your dad would go into a rage and you'd be so afraid, for example.

6. Child's Response:

What's the child's response on hearing the clinician's refusal to help their parent, i.e., hurt or anger/relief/resignation?
What's the child's feeling underlying the response?

7. Clinician's Response and Feeling:

Did shift occur?
What prompted the shift?
If not, what reinforced the block?
What is the clinician's plan going forward?
How did the clinician feel about the process? Any other observations from the process or debrief?

EFFT Processing Clinician Block Practice Sheet—Part I: Parental Involvement

As the therapist, ask your partner to think of a time when:

- You were angry with a parent or didn't want to invite them to the therapy
- Or felt hopeless about their ability to change or their ability to be able to help their client (child, adolescent, or adult client)

Switch

In the "other" chair (the chair on the right), picture yourself in the chair facing you:

- Be the part of you that blames the parent and tell yourself that (it's their fault because . . .)
- Or be the part of you that encourages you to protect the child from the parent's involvement (they will only make things worse . . .)
- Scare yourself by being explicit about what will happen and how that will be for you—as the clinician (you will look stupid, your team will judge you, things will get worse not better)
- Tell yourself what to do and why (avoid involving the parents, keep them out of treatment, it will be more effective without them)

Switch

In the "self" chair, picture the child in the "other" chair:

- Tell the child that you don't think their parent can help them
- Or tell the child that you don't like their parent—
- AND that, in fact, the parent is damaging to their progress and that you will be a better surrogate parent/that their parent is no good and will never change. Have the clinician say: "I will be a better mommy/daddy to you."

Switch

In the "other" chair, be the child:

- Tell the clinician what it's like for the child (sad, angry, relieved)
- As the child, what do you want the clinician to know? What do you need from the clinician in relation to your mom/dad? (to find a way of involving their parent, that they want and need their parent's help)

Copyright material from Mirisse Foroughe, 2018, *Emotion Focused Family Therapy with Children and Caregivers*, Routledge

- If as the child they feel anger or relief at not having parents involved, ask them to speak what is underneath the anger or relief (I want my mom/dad, I need you to find a way)

Switch

Ask them to tell you:
- What is it like to hear the child's response?
- What do you want to do for the child/the family?

   Tell the client the plan: e.g. I am going to arrange to see your parents; I will coach them about meal support, etc.

Switch

In the "other" chair, be the child
- How does the client respond? (happy/relieved/scared/doubtful)

EFFT Processing Clinician Block Practice Sheet—Part II: Feeling Incompetent/Discomfort With Emotion

As the therapist, ask your partner to:

- Identify a block related to feelings of incompetence/discomfort with emotion
  - they don't feel capable of doing this work
  - they are afraid to evoke strong emotion in their client

Switch

In the "other" chair:

- Be the part of you that tells you that you can't do this or that you shouldn't do this (you can't do this because . . .)
- Tell yourself how it will go badly for the client/family if you attempt to do this work/evoke emotion (that will only make things worse . . .)
- Scare yourself by being explicit about how that will be for you—as the clinician (you will look stupid, your team will judge you, things will get worse not better)
- Tell yourself what to do instead and why (stick to what you do, keep it light . . .)

Switch

In the "self" chair, picture the client in the "other" chair:

- Tell the client that you can't try these new techniques/go to the emotion in case it goes badly for them.
- Tell the client that you are also protecting yourself from what you indicated above:
  - ("I'm sorry I can't try these techniques. I'm just not good enough." or "I don't want to deepen your emotion because I'm scared I won't be able to handle it.")

Switch

In the "other" chair, be the client:

- Tell the clinician what it's like for the client (sad, angry, relieved)
- As the client, what do you want the clinician to know? What do you need from them? (they want you to find a way to help them; they need you to believe that they can go to the emotion)

Copyright material from Mirisse Foroughe, 2018, *Emotion Focused Family Therapy with Children and Caregivers*, Routledge

- If as the client they feel anger or relief at the clinician's decision, ask them to express what is underneath the anger or relief (I'm scared too but I need to do this)

Switch.

Ask them to tell you:
- What was it like to hear the client's response?
- What do you want to do for the client/the family?

Tell the client the plan: I am going to ...

Switch

In the "other" chair be the client
- How does the client respond? (happy/relieved/scared/doubtful)

EFFT Report: Don't Apologize Block—How To

Name of Client (e.g., parent/client/supervisee) _____
Date of Session _____
Father/Mother/Ex/Spouse/Grandparent

1. *Voice/Brain Boss Command:*

Don't apologize

2. *Client's Threat to Self:*

How does the person scare or threaten themselves into not apologizing, i.e., How does the self scare the self/How does the person's "voice" scare them? What do they tell themselves will go badly?

- If you apologize it means he gets away with what he did and it will feel so unfair, for example

3. *Client's Painful Feeling They Are Protecting Themselves From:*

What is the deep feeling underlying the client's refusal to apologize?
You will discover that you are to blame
You will realize that what you've been hanging onto all this time was false
You will lose the meaning or anchor you felt at defining the problem as THEM

4. *Child's Response to the Refusal to Apologize:*

What's the child's response on hearing the refusal to apologize, i.e., hurt or anger/relief/resignation?
What's the child's feeling underlying the response?

5. *Client Reaction to Child's Response:*

Did apology occur?
What prompted the shift?

6. *Reiterate the Don't Apologize and Validate It:*

What makes it feel so imperative to hold onto the bad feeling even in the face of the impact of holding onto resentment?

Copyright material from Mirisse Foroughe, 2018, *Emotion Focused Family Therapy with Children and Caregivers*, Routledge

What do they feel they will LOSE by "letting go" of resentment and/or of accepting responsibility?

- He doesn't deserve to be let off the hook
- You will discover that you are to blame
- You will realize that what you've been hanging onto all this time was false
- You will lose the meaning or anchor you felt at defining the problem as THEM

7. All Judgment Is Self-Judgment:

What things did that person do or not do that you didn't like or appreciate or that hurt you?
How did you show/convey your judgment of them when you were a child/pre-teen/teen, when you rebelled against/criticized them?
(Or if spouse or ex: when you were in the marriage with them, after you separated, or now if you are still with them?)
What was the look you put on their face?
Did they respond with feeling hurt/rejected or insulted/disrespected?

- e.g., you'll realize you really are a bad girl who doesn't deserve to be loved and that's why you were abandoned
- e.g., you will see how you hurt your parent with your judgment and how at your core you are unworthy
- e.g., remember the sad look on mom's face when you told her you hated her and she stayed in her room crying all day and left you alone?
- e.g., remember the angry look on dad's face when you told him that you rejected all of his values and he criticized you?

8. Debrief or Deepen:

Did apology occur?
What prompted the shift?
If not, when you deeply validated their inability to apologize now, what was their response?

Don't Apologize to Parent Practice Sheet

1) Starting with the client in the left chair, as the therapist, ask your partner to:

- Think of one of your parents who
  - treated you badly (didn't love you enough, left you, hurt you, etc.)
  - you do NOT believe you should apologize to for their shortcomings or problems they created for your family (e.g., leaving/divorcing, hurting you, being unavailable, being critical, etc.)

Switch

2) In the "other" chair (the chair on the right), picture yourself in the chair facing you:

- Be the part of you that tells yourself not to apologize to them (it's their fault because . . .)
- Scare yourself by being explicit about what will happen and how bad that will be for you if you do apologize
- Tell yourself what to do and why (hold your ground; don't give in; hold onto the grudge no matter what the consequences; don't forgive and certainly don't apologize)

Switch

3) In the "self" chair, first:

Picture your parent in the "other" chair:

- Tell them that you are never going to apologize and you will never forgive them
- AND that you are going to hold onto the bad feelings no matter what the price
- AND that you fully expect your own child(ren) never to forgive you and you accept that (if no children: AND that it's more important to you to hate them than to free yourself from this resentment)
- What do you see on your parent's face?

4) Still in the "self" chair, then:

Picture your child(ren) in the "other" chair (if no children, picture self at 80 years old):

- Tell them that you are never going to apologize to, or forgive, your parent/their grandparent

Copyright material from Mirisse Foroughe, 2018, *Emotion Focused Family Therapy with Children and Caregivers*, Routledge

- AND that you are going to hold onto the bad feelings no matter what the price
- AND that you fully expect them, your own child(ren), never to forgive you and you accept that (if no children: AND that it's more important to you to hate your ex than to free yourself and open up to love again)

Switch

5) In the "other" chair, be your child(ren) (or 80-year-old self)

- What happens? (sad, angry, rejecting, begging)
    - if angry, have them express what's underneath
- As the child, what do you want mom/dad to know? Tell them what you need from them regarding your grandparent.

> Note:
> Two critical points to get to apology: Realizing that you are holding onto the pain
> Realizing that you are feeding the pain to your child/80-year-old self

Switch

6) In the "self" chair, if apology occurs naturally:

Switch and have the parent respond, then have the child respond, then debrief.

If apology did NOT occur:
Reiterate the Don't Apologize and Validate It:

Switch

7) In the "other" chair, elicit statements from that part to the self: "Tell yourself...":

- What makes it feel so imperative to hold onto the bad feeling even in the face of the impact that holding onto resentment will have on their child (80-year-old self)?
- What will they LOSE by "letting go" of resentment and/or of accepting responsibility?

Copyright material from Mirisse Foroughe, 2018, *Emotion Focused Family Therapy with Children and Caregivers*, Routledge

- What identity or attachment injury be evoked/they be reminded of that they can't bear to revisit or feel?
    - e.g., you'll realize you really are a bad girl who doesn't deserve to be loved and that's why you were abandoned
    - e.g., you'll see how you hurt your parent with your judgment and how at your core you are unworthy
    - e.g., remember the sad look on mom's face when you told her you hated her and she stayed in her room crying all day and left you alone?
    - e.g., remember the angry look on dad's face when you told him that you rejected all his values and he criticized you?

All Judgment Is Self-Judgment:

Switch

8) *In the "self" chair:*

- Explore with them what the "self is holding against the self" in regard to the relationship with the other.
- What things did that person do or not do that you didn't like or appreciate or that hurt you?
- How did you show/convey your judgment of them as a child/pre-teen/teen when you rebelled against/criticized them?
- What was the look you put on their face?
- Did they respond with feeling hurt/rejected or insulted/disrespected?

9) *Still in the "self" chair, debrief or deepen:*

- If apology occurs naturally, do it.
- Debrief with the therapist.
- If not, switch one more time to the "other" chair, reiterate the don't apologize, then switch back to the "self" chair and deeply validate. (You just can't do it right now.)

> Note:
> Critical points in understanding radical responsibility and the apology:
> Becoming aware of the conversation in the other's head that you evoked and how that led to the other's reaction
> Realizing that resentment imprisons the SELF
> Realizing that taking responsibility and apologizing—letting go of judgment and restoring of compassion—is the road to freedom

Don't Apologize to Ex or Partner Practice Sheet

1) Starting with the client in the left chair, as the therapist, ask your partner to:

- Think of your ex (or your current partner) who treated you badly (didn't love you enough, left you, hurt you, etc.) and think of what specifically should you *not* apologize for (e.g., leaving/divorcing, hurting you, being unavailable, being critical, etc.).

Switch

2) In the "other" chair (the chair on the right), picture yourself in the chair facing you:

- Be the part of you that tells yourself not to apologize to them (it's their fault because . . .).
- Scare yourself by being explicit about what will happen and how bad that will be for you if you do apologize.
- Tell yourself what to do and why (hold your ground; don't give in; hold onto the grudge no matter what the consequences; don't forgive and certainly don't apologize).

Switch

3) In the "self" chair, first:

Picture that person (ex or partner) in the "other" chair:

- Tell them that you are never going to apologize and you will never forgive them
- AND that you are going to hold onto the bad feelings no matter what the price
- AND that it's more important to you to hate them than to free your children from the hate between you (if no children—than to open up to love again).
- What do you see on their face?

4) Still in the "self" chair, then:

Picture your child(ren) in the "other" chair (if no children, self at 80 years)

- Tell them that you are never going to apologize to, or forgive their parent (your ex)

Copyright material from Mirisse Foroughe, 2018, *Emotion Focused Family Therapy with Children and Caregivers*, Routledge

- AND that you are going to hold onto the bad feelings no matter what the price
- AND that it's more important to you to hate their other parent than to free them from the hate between you (if no children—to hate your ex than to open up to love again).

Switch

5) In the "other" chair, be your child(ren) (or 80-year-old self)

- What happens? (Are they sad, angry, rejecting, begging?)
    - if angry, have them express what's underneath
- As the child, what do you want mom/dad to know? Tell them what you need from them in regard to your other parent.

> Note:
> Two critical points to get to apology: Realizing that you are holding onto the pain
> Realizing that you are feeding the pain to the child/80-year-old self

Switch

6) In the "self" chair, if apology occurs naturally:

Switch and have the parent respond, then the child respond, then debrief.

If apology did NOT occur:
Reiterate the Don't Apologize and Validate It:

Switch

7) In the "other" chair, elicit statements from that part to the self:
"Tell yourself . . .":

- What makes it feel so imperative to hold onto the bad feeling even in the face of the impact on the child of holding onto resentment
- What they will LOSE by "letting go" of resentment and/or of accepting responsibility
- What identity or attachment injury or self-blame will be evoked/they be reminded of that they can't bear to revisit or feel

Copyright material from Mirisse Foroughe, 2018, *Emotion Focused Family Therapy with Children and Caregivers*, Routledge

- e.g., you'll realize you really are a bad girl who doesn't deserve to be loved, and that's why you were abandoned
- e.g., you'll see how you hurt that person with your judgment and how at your core you are unworthy
- e.g., remember how you let the kids side with you against their other parent when you shrunk back and called them mean
- e.g., remember the look of fear you put on their face when you got angry

All Judgment Is Self-Judgment:

Switch

8) In the "self" chair:

- Explore with them what the "self is holding against the self" in regard to the relationship with the other.
- What things did that person do or not do that you didn't like or appreciate or that hurt you?
- How did you show/convey your judgment of them, e.g., when you criticized them?
- What was the look you put on their face?
- Did they respond with feeling hurt/rejected or insulted/disrespected?

9) Still in the "self" chair, Debrief or Deepen:

- If apology occurs naturally, do it.
- Debrief with the therapist.
- If not, switch one more time to the "other" chair, reiterate the don't apologize, then switch back to "self" chair and deeply validate. (You just can't do it right now.)

Note:
Critical points in understanding radical responsibility and the apology:
Becoming aware of the conversation in the other's head that you evoked and how that led to the other's reaction
Realizing that resentment imprisons the SELF
Realizing that taking responsibility and apologizing—letting go of judgment and restoring of compassion—is the road to freedom

---

Copyright material from Mirisse Foroughe, 2018, *Emotion Focused Family Therapy with Children and Caregivers*, Routledge

EFFT Report: Clinician Block—Incompetent—How To

Name of Clinician _____ Date of Supervision Session _____

1. Brief Scenario:

One sentence to describe the context or situation of the block, e.g., clinician feels they can't try this approach or these techniques because they don't know it well enough.

2. Marker:

What does the clinician want to change or feel they should change but is not able or willing to do? OR

What does the supervisor see as problematic/needing change that the clinician is not able or willing to do? Or where does the supervisor feel the clinician is stopping themselves?

3. Voice/Brain Boss Command:

What does the clinician tell themselves to convince themselves not to do some particular thing with the client or family? To keep doing things the way they're doing them now? To keep themselves from changing their approach?

For example: Don't try this because you can't do it well enough and you will fail

4. Clinician's Threat to Self:

How does the clinician scare or threaten themselves into not trying?

That is, how does the self scare the self/How does the clinician's "voice" scare them? "If you try this . . ." What do they tell themselves will go badly?

For example: If you try it, you will fail.

5. Clinician's Painful Feeling They Are Protecting Themselves From:

What is the deep feeling underlying the clinician's scaring themselves?

For example: You will feel exposed as an impostor and as incompetent, and you will feel ashamed.

What childhood memory did the clinician use to remind themselves of that feeling? i.e., when they were vulnerable/abandoned/shamed; e.g., remember when your dad would say you should have done better even when you had a good grade.

Copyright material from Mirisse Foroughe, 2018, *Emotion Focused Family Therapy with Children and Caregivers*, Routledge

6. Client's Response:

What's the client's response on hearing the clinician's refusal to try to help them, i.e., hurt or anger/relief/resignation?

What's the client's feeling underlying the response?

7. Clinician's Response and Feeling:

Did shift occur?
What prompted the shift?
If not, what reinforced the block?
What is the clinician's plan going forward?
How did the clinician feel about the process? Any other observations from the process or debrief?

EFFT Validation Guidelines

		Negative	Positive
Validation Quadrant:	Invalidate	Be Negative Invalidate	Be Positive Invalidate
	Validate	Be Negative Validate	Just Validate Is It Positive or Negative?

Validation Guidelines:

- No *wonder* you feel that way
- Change BUT to BECAUSE ... No wonder you feel that way *because* ...
- Avoid going for the *bright side*
- Be aware of, then let go of, your agenda or investment in the issue (at least suspend it temporarily)

★★★Validate the EXPERIENCE as well as the feeling. For example, with a Learning Disability: It's not enough to say, "It's hard that you feel like you don't get it as fast as the other kids." No—it's true that they DON'T get it as fast! So we need to validate that, too. "It's so frustrating—your brain just doesn't work like all your friends when it comes to doing math. And that can make you feel like you're stupid" (if that's the word the loved one used!). Then eventually, after lots of validating, parent can find their way to bringing in what they ARE good at without it being invalidating: e.g., "And being 'good at art' just doesn't cut it when you're sitting there feeling like you aren't as smart as everyone else in math!"

Copyright material from Mirisse Foroughe, 2018, *Emotion Focused Family Therapy with Children and Caregivers*, Routledge

Validation Exercise

1. Exercise One—Part One:

Invalidate

Client tells the therapist the thing the child needs validated:

Client: "I don't like the dark-faced ones."
Therapist: Invalidate.

Switch roles.

Client: "I want to get up before everyone in the family."
Therapist: Invalidate.

2. Exercise One—Part Two:

Validate

Start again. Use the same statements as above.

Therapist: Validate.

Switch roles.

Therapist: Validate.

****Come Together With Group to Discuss****

3. Exercise Two—Part One:

Invalidate Anger

Client tells the therapist the EASY thing they identified in their homework that they feel or felt angry at.

Client: "I feel or felt angry at (person) for (thing)."
Therapist: Invalidate.

Switch roles.

Client: "I feel or felt angry at (person) for (thing)."
Therapist: Invalidate.

Copyright material from Mirisse Foroughe, 2018, *Emotion Focused Family Therapy with Children and Caregivers*, Routledge

4. Exercise Two—Part Two:
Validate Anger

Start again. Use the same statements as above.

Therapist: Validate.

Switch roles.

Therapist: Validate.

Parental Therapy-Interfering Behaviours

1. Identify a "style" of parent you've experienced (or heard about through their adolescent or adult child with whom you are working) who you would hesitate to involve in the treatment process.

- Critical of their loved one, their partner or the treatment team—or of you!
- Dismissive or in denial of their loved one's illness
- "Defensive" about being blamed
- Emotionally fragile
- Suffering from a serious mental health issue
- Doesn't want to be involved
- Is too busy to come in
- Lives too far away

2. On a scale of 1–10, rate the potential for this parent to play a positive and supportive role in their loved one's recovery. A lower number refers to a lower level of potential.

1 — 2 — 3 — 4 — 5 — 6 — 7 — 8 — 9 — 10

3. Identify a total of three therapy-interfering behaviours that you observe (or would expect the parent to engage in) during the session with their loved one or outside of the session:

A. Criticize you
B. Criticize the loved one
C. Cancel
D. Be aggressive in the session
E. Become blatantly distressed, tearful, beating self up
F. Align with the loved one in opposition to you
G. Insist that the loved one take the lead/take charge of the Symptom Interruption
H. Undermine or devalue therapy or team recommendations
I. Get angry or blow up in front of their loved one for having symptoms
J. Give up on supporting loved one in the face of resistance
K. Go against therapy or team recommendations re: behaviour
L. Say one thing in the session, not follow through outside
M. Give up on the possibility of recovery

4. In your opinion, what negative outcomes could happen if their loved one were exposed to, or continued to be exposed to, these behaviours:

- Not engage in the therapy
- Become more symptomatic

Copyright material from Mirisse Foroughe, 2018, *Emotion Focused Family Therapy with Children and Caregivers*, Routledge

- Become depressed, suicidal
- Become hopeless about family's potential to "get it" or change
- Become hopeless about their own potential to change if they feel they must align with the parent
- Devalue the therapy
- Not recover

5. Therapy-interfering behaviours serve to regulate fear, shame, helplessness, hopelessness, and/or resentment in the parent.

For each of the three therapy-interfering behaviours that you noted above (Question 3), check the emotions in the parent that might be driving the expression of their behaviours. Note which behaviour you identified in the blank (A, B, C, etc.) and check *all of the feelings that apply* for each of the identified behaviours.

Behaviour ——— *Fear, shame, helplessness, hopelessness, resentment*
Behaviour ——— *Fear, shame, helplessness, hopelessness, resentment*
Behaviour ——— *Fear, shame, helplessness, hopelessness, resentment*

1. Criticize you
2. Criticize the loved one
3. Cancel
4. Be aggressive in the session
5. Become blatantly distressed, tearful, beating self up
6. Align with the loved one in opposition to you
7. Insist that the loved one take the lead/take charge of the Symptom Interruption
8. Undermine or devalue therapy or team recommendations
9. Get angry or blow up in front of their loved one for having symptoms
10. Give up on supporting loved one in the face of resistance
11. Go against therapy or team recommendations re: behaviour
12. Say one thing in the session, not follow through outside
13. Give up on the possibility of recovery

6. What three negative outcomes could happen for *you* as the clinician if you were exposed to, or continued to be exposed to, these parental behaviours (observing them in session or hearing about them from your client):

a) Feel anger towards the parent
b) Dislike the parent
c) Feel incompetent

Copyright material from Mirisse Foroughe, 2018, *Emotion Focused Family Therapy with Children and Caregivers*, Routledge

d) Feel hopeless
e) Feel worried for the loved one
f) Lose the alliance with the loved one so feel like a bad therapist
g) Blame the parent
h) Feel burned out
i) Feel responsible for the further breakdown of the parent–child relationship

7. Reluctance to bring in the parent serves to regulate fear, shame, helplessness, hopelessness and/or resentment in the clinician.

For each of the negative outcomes you identified in Question 6, check the emotions that might be driving your reluctance to work with the identified parent. Check *all of those that apply* for each of the identified negative outcomes.

Negative outcome ———— Fear, shame, helplessness, hopelessness, resentment
Negative outcome ———— Fear, shame, helplessness, hopelessness, resentment
Negative outcome ———— Fear, shame, helplessness, hopelessness, resentment

8. Picture the child/client in front of you and visualize sharing with them the rating you gave in #2 along with the reasons you identified on the sheet for your rating.

"I think that your parent's capacity to be positive and supportive in your recovery is a _____ out of 10 (from question 2) because I think they will 1. _____, 2. _____, 3. _____ (from question 3).

a. Picture the child/client's reaction to your statement. What do you see on their face and feel in their body language in response? Check below the feelings they may be feeling:

Relief (if relief, which of the other emotions would they be left with)
Sadness
Helplessness
Hopelessness
Fear
Anger
Shame

b. What would they want you to know?

c. What would they want you to do?

Glossary

Adult Attachment Interview (AAI): A semi-structured interview developed by Carol George, Nancy Kaplan, and Mary Main that is used to identify an individual's attachment style. Individuals are asked to recall childhood memories of their relationships with caregivers and to reflect on how these early experiences may have impacted their adult personality and behaviour.

Affect Phobia: A fear of feelings. When faced with the possibility of experiencing the feared emotion, affect phobia can trigger a person's defences, which protect the individual by helping them avoid the possibility of experiencing the painful feeling(s) they fear.

Behaviour Therapy: A form of psychotherapy that applies principles of learning and conditioning to eliminate symptoms and modify ineffective or maladaptive patterns of behaviour. The focus is on the behaviour itself as well as factors in the environment that reinforce the behaviour rather than an exploration of the psychological causes of that behaviour.

Borderline Personality Disorder: In the DSM, this is a personality disorder characterized by a longstanding pattern of instabilities in mood, relationships, and self-image that is severe enough to cause extreme distress or interfere with social and occupational functioning.

Cognitive Behaviour Therapy (CBT): A form of psychotherapy that integrates theories from cognition and learning with treatment techniques derived from cognitive therapy and behaviour therapy. CBT assumes that cognitive, emotional, and behavioural variables are functionally interrelated and treatment is aimed at identifying and modifying the clients' maladaptive thought processes and problematic behaviours to achieve positive change.

Cognitive: Derived from the noun cognition, which refers to all forms of knowing and awareness such as perceiving, conceiving, remembering, reasoning, judging, imagining, and problem solving. It is one of three traditionally identified components of the mind.

Deactivating Strategies: Used by individuals with a dismissing style to minimize or altogether avoid difficult attachment-related memories and emotions in order to protect themselves from psychological pain and rejection.

Defensive Exclusion: A psychological process of selectively attending to information and/or defensively excluding memories to protect oneself from painful attachment-related experiences and to preserve a positive image and faith in one's parents. Examples include difficulty recalling specific childhood memories and the idealization of an abusive parent.

Dismissing (Avoidant) Attachment: An attachment style characterized by the avoidance of emotion and closeness in relationships. Individuals who are dismissing of attachment tend to view and portray themselves as independent, self-sufficient, and invulnerable to feelings associated with attachment. They deal with painful emotions and rejection through avoidance and distancing.

Distancing Manoeuvre: Triggered by their fear of vulnerability, individuals with a dismissing attachment style often distance themselves from relationships that have grown too intimate, including the therapeutic relationship. For example, a client may "forget" to show up to a session or may work hard to keep the session's focus at a surface level, avoiding emotional and attachment-related content.

Ego-Syntonicity: Refers to the state of having behaviours, values, and feelings that are in harmony with, or acceptable to, the needs and goals of the self. Consistent with one's ideal self-image.

Emotional Needs: Refers to the specific set of needs that a particular emotion triggers. For example: fear needs reassurance, anger needs boundaries, and sadness needs comfort.

Emotion Regulation: The ability of an individual to modulate an emotion or set of emotions. Emotion regulation typically increases across the lifespan.

Empathy: Understanding a person from his or her frame of reference rather than one's own, so that one vicariously experiences the person's feelings, perceptions, and thoughts.

Enabling Behaviours: A process whereby someone unwittingly or knowingly contributes to continued maladaptive behaviour in another person.

Evidence-Based Practices (EBP): The integration of the best available scientific research from laboratory and field settings with clinical expertise so as to provide effective psychological services that are responsive to culture, preferences, and characteristics. In uniting researchers and practitioners, EBP ensures that the research on psychological assessment, case formulation, intervention, therapeutic relationships, and outcomes is both clinically relevant and internally valid. The ultimate goal of EBP is to promote empirically supported principles that can be used to enhance public health.

Frightened/Frightening Behaviour: Parental behaviours that give away a parent's fear of their child and may be experienced by the child as frightening. Examples include frightened facial expressions or voice tone, role reversals, and dissociative behaviours.

Instrumental Emotions: Strategic displays of emotion for their intended effect on others, either expressed deliberately out of habit or automatically without full awareness.

Interdependence: When two or more people rely on each other, not only for practical help, but for emotional support as well. Interdependence can engender a sense of vulnerability as it requires trust, and is therefore avoided by individuals with a dismissing attachment style.

Intergenerational Transmission: Refers to the passing of trauma and attachment insecurity from one generation to the next through the parent-child relationship. Less than optimal patterns of parenting are sometimes repeated within families and across generations.

Internalizing: Behaviours characterized primarily by processes within the self such as anxiety, somatization, and depression.

Internal Working Model: A mental framework, based on early attachment experiences, that guides a person's understanding of the world, themselves, and others, and which influences their expectations of and responses to current relationships.

Intrafamilial Trauma: Refers to a type of complex trauma involving interpersonal or relational disturbances within the family context, including salient instances of child abuse (e.g., sexual or physical abuse and/or observing domestic violence) as well as more subtle or hidden forms of trauma (e.g., parental unavailability, emotional abuse, and neglect).

Literature Review: An evaluative report of information found in the academic literature related to a selected area of study. A review should describe, summarize, evaluate, and clarify the existing literature and should give a theoretical base for the research to help the author determine the nature and direction of the research.

Marker: A specific in-session client state that signals an underlying affective-cognitive processing problem.

Maladaptive: Not providing adequate or appropriate adjustment to the environment or situation.

Minimization: A deactivation strategy whereby a person downplays or disregards the emotional significance, long-term impact, and/or negative effect or severity of trauma and attachment-related experiences.

Motivational Interviewing: A client-centred directive approach for facilitating change by helping people to resolve ambivalence and find intrinsic reasons for making a needed change. Particularly applicable when low internal motivation for change is an obstacle. Rather than advocating and suggesting methods for change, this approach seeks to elicit the client's own goals, values, and motivation for change.

Over-Responding: When a parent responds to normal (although sometimes overly sensitive and intense) child emotion or behaviour in a way that pathologizes the child. For example, a parent might respond in an overly negative or intense way relative to the situation.

Primary Adaptive Emotions: Emotional responses that are a person's first, natural reactions to the current situation that would help them take appropriate action.

Primary Emotions: A person's most fundamental, direct initial reactions to a situation.

Primary Maladaptive Emotions: Emotional responses that occur repeatedly and do not shift in response to changing circumstance. They do not provide adaptive directions for solving problems when they are experienced.

Problematic Reaction Point: A marker that is observed when the client expresses puzzlement or confusion about their emotional or behavioural response to a situation.

Psychoeducation: Refers to the process of providing education and information to those seeking or receiving mental health services and their family members.

Secondary Emotions: Responses to a person's own primary emotions, rather than to the situation.

Self-Efficacy: An individual's capacity to act effectively to bring about a desired result, especially as perceived by the individual.

Self-Interruptive Split: A marker that is observed when the client constricts emotional experience or expression—i.e., doesn't allow themselves to feel something.

Self-Organization: Also referred to as "spontaneous order"; a process where some form of overall order arises from local interactions between parts of an initially disordered system. The process is spontaneous, not needing control by an external agent.

Task: An empirically validated intervention indicated by a given client marker.

Transdiagnostic: Refers to treatments that apply the same underlying principles across mental disorders without tailoring the protocol to a specific diagnosis.

Treatment Protocol: The formal procedures used in a system of psychotherapy. In some systems, few explicit rules apply, whereas in others, strict adherence to a treatment protocol is often used to guide the work of the therapist.

Unclear Felt Sense: A marker that is observed when the client is on the surface of a particular experience, feels confused, and is unable to get a clear sense of the experience.

Unfinished Business: A marker that is observed when the client makes a statement that shows lingering unresolved feelings toward a significant other, in a highly involved manner.

Unresponsiveness: Occurs when a child needs support and the parent is unable to provide this support because of their own blocks. For example, a parent may fail to set limits or may not respond to his or her child's distress by providing comfort.

Index

Page numbers in italic indicate a figure and page numbers in bold indicate a table on the corresponding page.

activate and challenge strategy 100
adaptive emotional response 3–4, 7
Adelson, E. 104
Adult Attachment Interview (AAI) 105
affect phobia 109
anger: as adaptive response 3, 15; assertiveness 39; blast, as therapy response 25; to cover emotions 27; empty-chair dialogue and 30; maladaptive shame and 6; in self-critical split work 24; superfeelers and 72; unfinished business and 9
Animal Models 51
anti-caregiver messaging 68
attachment avoidance 23–24, 33
attachment based family therapy (ABFT) 23–24, 31–32
attachment behaviour 104–105
attachment insecurity *81*
attachment-related memories 24
attunement 63, 67, 84, 113
Auszra, L. 5
avoidance 104–106; *see also* dismissive attachment style
awareness, emotional 4

blast, as therapy response 25, 27, 75
blocker chair 90–91
blocks *see* emotional blocks
Boachie, A. 67
body sculpting 90
bonding and awareness phase of EFT 6–7
Bowlby, J. 104–105

caregivers: anti-caregiver messaging 68; emotion coaching and 49; parent blocks workshop 91–97; preparing child for parent involvement 33–35; processing blocks 90–91; stress of 67; supporting behavioural recovery 48; with trauma history 29–30; workshop delivery 76–78; *see also* families, parents
cascading attunement 63, 84
chair work: blocker chair 90–91; in context of EFFT 57–59; empty-chair dialogue 10, 14–15; engaging in the process 75–76; parent blocks and 86–87; for processing blocks 91–97; two-chair dialogue 8–9, 11–14, 24, 52–53, 55–57
child and family treatments: accessing core maladaptive feelings 37–38; confidentiality and 65; co-parenting sessions 40–41; de-pathologizing the child 67, 72; individual parent sessions 39–40; maintenance 38–39; parental emotion in process 66–67; parent-child dyadic for 35–41; parent-child sessions 38; separating parent and child sessions 36–37; stabilization 36–37; umbrella approach 39
child emotion work 24–29
client-centered empathic treatment 1
clinician anxiety 54–55
clinician blocks 54–57
Clinician Drift Model 54
cognitive behavioural therapy (CBT) focus of eating disorder treatment programs 46
confidentiality 33–34, 65–66
conflict splits 8–9
co-parenting sessions 40–41
core components of EFFT: emotion coaching 48–50; processing emotional blocks 50–51; recovery coaching 48; relationship repair 50

deactivating strategies 99–100, 101, 104–106
de-blaming 66–67
debriefing an emotional session 112–113
defensive strategies **106–107**
denial, as therapy response 25–26
de-pathologizing the child 67, 72
depression 1
Diamond, G. S. 23, 33
dismissive attachment style 99–104, 116–117
distancing manoeuvres 113–115
Dolhanty, J. 23, 45–46
"Don't Apologize" exercise 87–89

eating disorders 23, 45–46
EFT Kids case series 32–35
emotional blocks: clinician blocks 54–57; definition of 80; parent blocks 51–54; processing 50–51; processing in workshop setting 90–91; psychoeducation and 89–90; significance of 80–81; survival-based origin of 80–81; validating 81–82
emotional change, principles of 4–6
emotional expression, facilitating 26
emotional memories 2
emotional processing 4, 23–24, 31–32, 37
emotional safety 109
emotional sensitivities 102
emotional transformation 5–7
emotion avoidance 70–71
emotion coaching 48–50, 71, 74
emotion diagnostic system 3
emotion focused family therapy: clinical illustration of 72–75; definition of 59; integrating EFT and 57–59; integrating into practice 76–78; targeting core emotions 69–70; teaching steps of 72–75; workshops 76–78
emotion-focused therapy: attachment based family therapy vs. 31–32; case example 11–18; integrating EFFT and 57–59; phases of 6–7; umbrella treatment 41–42
emotion-minimization 108–109
emotions: awareness 4–5; components of 70–71; connected to essential needs 2; definition of 70; engaging in the process 75–76; expression 4–5; as foundation for cognitive processes 2; instrumental 4; maladaptive 5; positive 5–6; primary 3; as primary

communication system 70; reflection 5; regulation 5; secondary 3; types of 3–4
emotion schemes 2–3, 16
empathic validation 10
empathy 85–86, 113
empty-chair dialogue 10, 14–15
evoking and exploring phase of EFT 7
experiencing self 11–12
experiential engagement 2
expression, emotional 4–5

families *see* caregivers, parents
fear-based difficulties 24
felt emotions 2
felt sense 8
focusing intervention 8
Fraiberg, S. 104
Franko, D. L. 54
Frederickson, B. 5–6

Gottman, J. 49
Greenberg, L. S. 5, 23, 36

Heart of Parenting, The: Raising an Emotionally Intelligent Child (Gottman) 49
Herrmann, I. R. 5
Herzog, D. B. 54

Iatrogenic Maintenance Model 54
individual child therapy, EFT in 24–29
insecure attachment 102
instrumental emotions 4
intergenerational transmission of attachment and insecurity 81, 82–83, 103
intergenerational trauma 81
interventions, markers and 7–10
intervention strategies 63, 107–115
intrafamilial trauma 29

Jasper, K. 67
Johnson, Sue 23

Kosmerly, S. 54

Lafrance Robinson, A. 45–46, 54
Lieberman, M. D. 4
lifetime learning model 57

maladaptive coping strategies 70–71
maladaptive emotions 5
markers: case example of 11–18; interventions and 7–10

McHale Co-Parenting Scale 40
misattunement 75, 82, 102
most vulnerable parents 78
motivational interviewing 46

Neonatal Intensive Care Unit (NICU) 68
New Maudsley's Animal Models 51

O'Brien, K. 68

parent blocks: case example of 86–87; defensive strategies **106–107**; interfering with treatment 84–86; processing 86–87; recognizing 83–84; relationship repair and 51–54; to setting limits 84–85; to showing empathy 85–86; types of 84–86
parent-child dyads 35–41, 46
parent coaching 59, 89–90
Parenting Dimensions handout 85–86
parent preparation sessions 34–35
parents: as central treatment of child 99; confidentiality and 65; as critical partners in care 59; de-blaming 67, 69; with dismissive attachment style 100–104; emotional styles of 47; in emotion-focused therapeutic process 30–31; emotions interfering with caregiver efforts 50–51; empowering 67–68; enabling illness 47; engaging in the process 64; involving in child's therapy 30–31; peripheral involvement in child's treatment 46; self-blame 48; working with most vulnerable 78; *see also* caregivers, families
Pos, A. E. 36
positive emotions 5–6
primary adaptive emotion responses 3–4, 15
primary emotions 3
primary maladaptive emotions 3–4, 15
problematic reaction marker 7–8

processing, definition of 80
psychoeducation and processing blocks 89–90

recovery coaching 48, 74
reflection, emotional 5
regulation, emotional 5
relationship repair 50, 74, 88
Robinson, A. 23

Satir, D. A. 54
Schmidt, U. 47
secondary emotions 3
self-blame 37, 40, 48, 76, 78, 88
self-critical splits 8–9, 24
self-interruptive splits 9
Shapiro, V. 104
silence, as therapy response 27
stabilization 36–37
successful task resolution in individual child therapy 25
superfeelers 72, 101
symptom interruption 74

therapeutic change 2, 4, 100
Thompson-Brenner, H. 54
transformation *see* emotional transformation
transformation, emotional 87
transmission of intergenerational trauma and attachment insecurity *81*
trauma history, involving caregivers with 29–30
trauma-informed therapy 77
Treasure, J. 47
two-chair dialogue 8–9, 11–14, 24, 52–53, 55–57

umbrella treatment 39, 41–42, *42*
unfinished business 9–10, 16, 24–29

vulnerability 10, 78, 113